Cold Comfort

ALSO BY GIL McELROY

POETRY

Dream Pool Essays*

Last Scattering Surfaces*

NonZero Definitions*

Ordinary Time*

Some Julian Days

The Merton Lake Propers

ART CRITICISM

Gravity & Grace: Selected Writing on Contemporary Canadian Art

*Available from Talonbooks

COLD COMFORT

GROWING UP COLD WAR

Gil McElroy

TALONBOOKS

Talonbooks
P.O. Box 2076
Vancouver, British Columbia, Canada V6B 3S3
www.talonbooks.com

Typeset in Minion and printed and bound in Canada.
Printed on 100% post-consumer recycled paper.
Typeset and cover design by Typesmith.

First printing: 2012

The publisher gratefully acknowledges the financial support of the Canada Council for the Arts; the Government of Canada through the Canada Book Fund; and the Province of British Columbia through the British Columbia Arts Council and the Book Publishing Tax Credit for our publishing activities.

LIBRARY AND ARCHIVES CANADA CATALOGUING IN PUBLICATION

McElroy, Gil

Cold comfort : growing up Cold War / Gil McElroy.
Includes bibliographical references and index.
ISBN 978-0-88922-684-5

1. McElroy, Gil—Childhood and youth. 2. McElroy, Don. 3. Children of military personnel--Canada--Biography. 4. Poets, Canadian (English)—Biography. 5. Radar defense networks—Canada—History. 6. DEW Line—History. 7. Cold War—Biography. 8. Canada, Northern—History, Military—20th century. 9. Canada, Northern—Biography. I. Title.

UG612.5.C3M34 2012 355.1 C2012-901617-9

for Heather
ever

If I am going to have a true memory,
there are a thousand things that must be forgotten.

– THOMAS MERTON
New Seeds of Contemplation

Behind the Iron Curtain
There is a piece of glass
And if you sit upon it
You'll hurt your little –
Ask me no more questions ...

– TRADITIONAL CHILDREN'S RHYME

CONTENTS

INTRODUCTION

Sorrow has a shape.

We – the family comprising my father, my mother, my sisters Elizabeth, Danielle, and Renee, and me – owned it, carried it with us from one side of a continent to the other and then halfway back again before sorrow (before this particular shape of it, anyway) became separated from our lives.

Sorrow looks like this: it's a glass bottle, green with a grid pattern of ridges that encircle it till halfway up from the base, where the form then swells outward before eventually tapering down to a lip at the top. It was manufactured to be held comfortably in the hand, to be carried about, to keep its contents cold, and to be drunk from. Imprinted onto its side is a small yellow banner through which the word "Wink" appears in the transparent green of the bottle. Above it is a logo, "Canada Dry."

Sorrow is a soft-drink bottle that, for many years, my mother used while ironing clothes. A small, dented metal sprinkler head with a corked neck fit tightly into its top, and as she ironed she would periodically shake the bottle, sprinkling the clothes on the board with water.

Decades on, I can still hear the sounds of the bottle being shaken, clothing being wetted. I hear the hiss of the iron meeting dampened cloth, the board beneath it creaking in time to my mother's motions, the plunk of the upright iron set at one end as she moved shirt or pants to another position and then did it all over again.

I give sorrow this shape, because this glass bottle was for me a primary link to my family's life as itinerants. This bottle, this *thing*, held my family together through moves from one side of a continent to the other, and then halfway back again. This bottle – this *thing*, its shape, colour, and the sound it made as it was shaken over top of wrinkled clothing, and the hiss of steam that immediately followed – carried us along together. As we moved about the country from one place to another, so many other things had to be left behind out of sheer necessity – a cleaving familiar to anyone who has ever experienced itinerancy on any scale, familial or otherwise – but the bottle persisted, carrying us along with it safely from one place to the next.

Now it's long gone. I haven't seen it in decades – my last memory of it would be from the early 1970s and our third home in the city of North Bay, Ontario – and at some level I persist in linking the fracturing of my family with its disappearance from our lives. Surely I'm wrong; surely its vanishing didn't coincide with my father's disappearance from our family.

Not that it matters. Remembrance of course has no formal shape, and so ultimately none of this can be true. Maybe I assign too much importance to a stupid glass bottle – likely discarded by my mother without hesitation as she acquired a brand-new steam iron that didn't require a separate tool to wet clothing – as if this thing could somehow influence the course of events in such a profound way.

And yet there is a real persistence, here, for the memory of this bottle and its utile sounds as my mother put it through its paces are inextricably woven into the fabric of my childhood and adolescent memories. They bridge numerous disparate homes and cities and even countries, and a good chunk of a war that really wasn't and which we therefore called Cold.

I mourn its loss. My sorrow has a shape.

~

In the beginnings of virtually any human relationship, there are two questions that are inevitably asked as you are sized up and a determination made as to the potential of your friendship value or mere usefulness in enabling that person to achieve some end: (1) "What do you do" (meaning: what job do you have); and (2) "Where are you from?" I intensely dislike answering the first question, preferring to try and keep myself out of the tiny, confining box of such assignation for as long as possible (I have learned not to make the all-too-common mistake of confusing what someone does for a living with who they are as a person), and so usually opt for saying something vague. But the second question is the one I struggle with most. Where *am* I from? I don't know how to answer. I was born in France, but in no way am I French. And besides, to answer the aforementioned question thusly sounds like I'd be trying too hard to be colourful and exciting when, in fact, I am neither.

So how do I answer? I lived the longest continuous chunk of my life in the northeastern Ontario city of North Bay, but I wasn't born there and, as much as the place became ingrained in me, I've never felt I was "from there." It's never felt like what I imagine "home" should feel like, even though I struggled for years hoping to make it so (or maybe fooling myself into believing that's what I wanted).

So how *do* I answer? "I'm a military brat," I tend to say, and most people nod either knowingly or in simple acknowledgement, and then the conversation – if it continues at all – tends to move on to some even more innocuous subject.

Maybe I overthink this, but to me it's an important question and deserves an honest answer that is as true as I can make it. I'm a brat – a military brat. *That's* where I come from. I grew up military. I grew up air force.

And I grew up Cold War.

I'm a baby boomer, part of that enormous swelling of children born in the post–World War II era that lasted into the 1960s. Born in 1956, I fall pretty much in the middle of that bulge of humanity, like a kind of statistical median.

At the more focused, intimate level of the family, though, I'm the privileged one, the first-born of my family, and the only male of the four children my parents had.

My North American–born father was himself the child of privileged WASPs – White, Anglo-Saxon, Protestants – and my less-privileged European mother is French and German. My parents met because of World War II and the Cold War that consequently ensued. As a military man, my father was a formal part of both conflicts. In contrast, my mother was a member of that enormous class of human beings referred to as "non-combatants." She witnessed firsthand that mid-century carnage we casually call World War II as it all played out in northeastern France near the city of Metz, then came of age herself in the postwar geopolitical rearrangements we've long called the Cold War that included the presence of a Royal Canadian Air Force base near where she lived, to which my father was posted, and because of which they met.

I say that I grew up air force, and that I grew up Cold War. Note that I'm not saying that I "grew up *in* the air force," or that I grew up "*in* the Cold War." This wasn't some kind of a metaphorical bath in which we immersed ourselves; this was who we were and even still are. The preposition "in" bothers me enormously, reeking of some kind of untruth, as if we – as if I – were some *thing* drifting unattached through a space and time of which I really wasn't a part. That's not so. As with a lot of other children, the Cold War generated me. I was born because of it; my parents encountered one another for no reason other than the fact that the Cold War brought them to a particular place and time in and around the city of Metz, France. In about May 1955 I was conceived, and at about the same time (in the larger, more importantly historical scheme), West Germany became a part of the North Atlantic Treaty Organization – NATO for short – and the Warsaw Pact of Eastern bloc countries was consequently formed in response. The particulars of that conjunction – my parents having sex and conceiving me, I mean – are no one else's business, not even mine. But the consequences most certainly are, for I was born on February 19, 1956, in northeastern France, smack dab in the middle of a war that wasn't an actual war as had been understood up until that time, but which affected absolutely everything in my life from my conception to my adulthood. So a rephrasing is in order: as it was for so many other kids, military or otherwise, the Cold War was the air that I breathed, the food that I ate, the places that I lived, the things that I knew, what I believed. And more, it was everything that, for good and for ill, I have become.

Being born in the mid-1950s meant that I wasn't around for the infancy of the Cold War, arguably born in the Yalta and later Potsdam Conferences held in 1945, during which the United States, the Union of Soviet Socialist Republics (U.S.S.R.), Great Britain, and France, politically carved up postwar Europe among themselves. It was nurtured by the late 1945 atomic incineration of the Japanese cities of Hiroshima and Nagasaki that gave impetus to a postwar arms race, and set to walking and talking in 1947 with the Truman Doctrine of intended U.S. containment of communist expansion around the globe.

I entirely missed experiences like the combinatory ridiculousness and terror of duck-and-cover drills taught at schools as a response to possible nuclear attack. Those drills now live on in old black-and-white civil emergency instructional films, often shown stripped of context to generate an easy laugh, as if curling up into a ball beneath your desk or against a brick wall could somehow afford you shelter from the effects of thermonuclear Armageddon. Thankfully, I wasn't privy to such antics; they were all before my time. But bomb shelters, which during a particularly touchy time of the Cold War people were encouraged to build, were very much a part of what I remember growing up. And in hindsight, they were as equally ridiculous and ultimately pointless as any duck-and-cover drill.

For the most part, my Cold War experience was of the everyday stuff. Sure, I had the living daylights scared out of me on more than one occasion by something of potentially global impact (the Cuban Missile Crisis of October 1962, for example, or for the adult me, something as recent as a 1983 shooting down of a Korean Air Lines Flight 007 by Soviet interceptor jets). But by and large, my terror was more of the mundane sort – maybe more like a super-elevated form of stress. Better yet, anxiety. Yeah, that's right: anxiety.

Living Cold War was living at a critical balance, anxiously teetering on a kind of knife's edge. The blade in this metaphor may've been sharp and cutting, but a worse fate would be falling off it entirely and plunging into the unknown. Maybe civilians could try to wish away or just ignore the Cold War. But wishing or ignoring was harder to do growing up military. We lived in a state of constant reminder. It was all around us, from the uniforms that most males and a heck of a lot of females of the military context of my childhood wore, to the kind of housing we lived in, to the air-raid sirens, the radar domes, air strips, fighter jets, missiles …

Listing it makes it feel like it's getting the psychological better of me now, like a vestigial echo of an old panic as too much was heaped on someone (that would be me) too young and consequently too incapable of simply shrugging it all off and moving on – if that was even possible. There are pictures I have of this kind of life, photo mementos from our various military postings. I'm even in some of them. I smile for the camera not because I necessarily wanted to, but because I did what I was told. I followed orders. There were no options, except maybe the possibly immediate repercussions of my father's belt on my behind, or the larger one of all of us falling off the knife's edge.

~

Despite all the me in this narrative so far, this memoir is ostensibly about my father, Donald Harrison McElroy – Don or Mac to the people he worked with, a heck of a lot of whom apparently knew him much better than his own family – and his experiences in the military. Like so many of his generation, my father joined up during World War II (in his case, the Royal Canadian Air Force) and served at various remote radar bases hastily established on the Canadian West Coast. After leaving it for several years when the war ended, he returned to make it a career. His consequent military and then post-military career (in which he worked for the military in all but name), virtually spans the entirety of the Cold War, from its beginnings in the years immediately following World War II and continuing to 1989 and the collapse of the Iron Curtain.

My father took pictures of nearly all of it. In what is called an Attestation Paper completed when he first enlisted in 1942, one of the questions posed to applicants was "Special Qualifications, Hobbies, etc., useful to the R.C.A.F." As his response, my father wrote just two words: "amateur photography."

This, then, is what this book is largely built around: my father's photographs. It's so because he was a man of few words. Parsimonious with his language (when I once showed him examples of the writing I was publishing about visual art and asked what he thought of it, he said that I was like my grandfather, using two words where one would have sufficed), he was equally parsimonious with the stories he told his children. There were moments when he did tell my sisters and me *some* stories about his life, but they constituted an exception to the rule, and by and large the person my father was has remained an utter mystery to us.

So this is where photographs matter – a lot. For a man who began taking pictures back in the 1930s right up until just a few years before his death in 1998, we (his children) saw surprisingly few of them. He was, it seems, equally parsimonious in sharing images as he was in sharing words with us. The bulk of his images remained out of view to us until after his death. It was then that I was given a series of numbered and dated slide carousels, and a mess of unsorted black-and-white prints and negatives in a beaten-up old cardboard container. The box. No, that doesn't do it justice. Let's call it "*The Box*." Most of the print images it contained had no information on the back, and one – only one – contained a bit of handwritten information that was tantalizing enough for me to embark upon this journey to try and find out just who this person that was my mostly absent father had been. The Box would be at my side all the way through.

Here are some of the broader contextual strokes: my father's adult life and career were inextricably bound to the development and implementation of the electronic defence of North America. With few exceptions, throughout that time he took pictures of the environments – military and otherwise – in which he worked and lived. Some of his images – especially the earliest – indeed constitute some of the surprisingly little visual evidence of just how Canada went about establishing an electronic early-warning system known as Chain Home as protection from feared German and Japanese attack during World War II, and then how the Canadian Arctic first began to be seriously militarized as the Cold War took shape in the late 1940s.

I'm not trying to make a case that my father was instrumental in helping create or shape any of this. He was, indeed, little more than a bit player, in many ways just along for the proverbial ride. Never an officer, he rose in the ranks no further than that of an NCO (Non-Commissioned Officer), achieving his highest rank as a Master Warrant Officer a year before his retirement from the Royal Canadian Air Force and only just after the powers-that-be politically erased the distinctions and boundaries between the branches of the Canadian military – army, air force, navy – in the late 1960s and rebranded it simply as the Canadian Forces (a decision that, like so many military people of the time, he absolutely detested). He was of no real historical significance outside his family, but I would argue that he contributed something vital to the historical record: he bore witness.

My father was there as history happened and he took pictures of some of it. He learned his military skills at what had been the very first radar school in the world, an institution located in rural Canada and which was so secret at the time that he took no pictures of it while he was posted there. His wartime images appeared when he became a part of Canada's first system of radar defence during World War II and he started photographing his isolated surroundings and some of the people with whom he served. He was there in the late 1940s when the United States and Canada first began to implement a military strategy for the Canadian Arctic, and he took pictures of the place and people who were a part of it. In the 1950s and 60s, he did tours of duty on the three major networks of the Cold War defence of North America: the Pinetree, Mid-Canada, and DEW Lines, all of which stretched the extent of the continent from the Pacific to the Atlantic and along the Arctic shores of North America, and all of which are now long gone and scarcely remembered.

It all bears repeating: my father sat on isolated bits of rocky islands on the Pacific Coast and stared at early and primitive radar screens keeping an eye out for a feared Japanese surprise attack on mainland North America during World War II. In the 1950s and early 60s, as the then-new digital computer created a truly coordinated continent-wide early warning system of defence, he kept watch at North American sites for a Soviet nuclear first strike from across the North Pole. He kept watch from France during the heyday of what came to be called the Iron Curtain that divided the democracies of Western Europe from the Soviet-dominated countries to the east. And to top it all off, over the course of three decades he worked on the northernmost line of electronic defence high in the Canadian Arctic, until the demise of the Iron Curtain and the eventual collapse of the Union of Soviet Socialist Republics in the early 1990s made it all obsolete.

A lot of people worked the DEW Line. By no means did participating in any of this history make my father unique or historically important. But he kept a kind of record through it all, taking photographs to document what went on around him and, in his earliest military days, hanging on to other images given him by fellow airmen (and possibly women). The bulk of it is innocuous, everyday snapshots of people smiling for the camera or involved in mundane kinds of activities. But a good chunk of it has meaning and importance, for it tells the story of how the Cold War shaped us psychologically and socially. It provides context.

My father's death in 1998 gave me permission to finally try and learn something of the man, whom I barely knew during his lifetime. No, that's not really true; "permission" isn't the right word at all. It gave me freedom – freedom from the fear of my father's judgment, an emotional and psychological space in which I could freely move and make mistakes, fumble and backtrack, and follow paths down to dead ends without being taken to task for my failures from the man who was quick to do so. My father's ability and willingness to judge me was pretty much all I knew about this person whose DNA , like it or not, is genetically engrained in me, and whom, it turns out, I am so very much like in many, many ways.

I loved my father, but let "love" not be confused with "like"; the living man was someone with whom I was never comfortable. He was someone I feared, even dreaded. He was absent for big chunks of my life while my sisters and I were growing up, and when he was around he was unavailable save for the well-placed caustic remark about something I'd said or done. My dead father, in contrast, has been so much easier to deal with. His passing at age seventy-six made his life ironically and finally available, something I could probe and inquire into without fear of repercussion. I figured all or most of it could be found within the emotionally manageable confines of The Box. Or so I hoped.

The Box, then, became my desk-side companion as I set about scouring through the photographic prints, negatives, and slides it held as I tried to get some sense of what this man had done with his life. Most of what I learned has been hard-won news. My father's reticence about what he had done in his life – about his childhood and adolescence growing up in relative affluence in Depression-era Windsor, Ontario; about the young adulthood of his pre-family military postings when, like so many of his generation, he signed on to take part in Canada's contribution to fighting World War II; or even about his life and experiences when he had a wife and children in tow – all of it made for tough going. I had some landmarks to guide me, for despite his taciturnity, he would hint, occasionally, of military matters he couldn't speak openly about. For example, in the mid-1960s, during a posting in the United States, he purchased and carefully built the first model kit made available of the SR-71 Blackbird, a super-secret American spy plane. Even as a child, I knew that, while he was a real aficionado of military airplanes, *this* model had something to do with those military secrets. Yet I think my father's job requirement to keep silent served him as a convenient mask to speak of nothing at all. His reticence and my fear of him sealed the deal. I would, in fact, grow up knowing practically nothing about him.

So this may be a book about my father's life, and about his photographs, but I suppose it's largely about his enigma. And how do you write about something you know almost nothing about? There's educated guesswork, of course, most of it based on whatever the hell was going on in the world at a particular time, for much of it would have had a fairly direct impact on what my father would be doing.

I've made a few surprising discoveries in the process. My father loved to fly, for instance, and many of his few revelations about his life had to do with airplanes. But during his three years of service during World War II, and despite the facts that he (a) was a member of the Royal Canadian Air Force, and (b) served during that period in some pretty remote locations, he never set foot in an airplane (actually, not until he rejoined the military several years after the end of the war). His World War II was vehicular – cars, trucks, and trains – and marine (converted fishing boats actually turned out to be the only means of travel between his isolated wartime postings). A careful scanning of his postwar re-enlistment papers revealed this tiny little bit of, what was for me, unexpected information that contradicted the paradigm I'd built around the man.

But contradictions abound, here, for while this is a book about my father, and a book about photography, in the end it's really a book about growing up in the shadow of an enigma. The Cold War may have shaped how I would respond to the world (usually involving some form of fear), but the darkness of unknowing cast across my life by my father is utterly personal. He was no geopolitical abstraction. He was intimate flesh I feared and yet whose approval and love I craved.

Still do.

1

BEFORE THE WAR

This is what I know of my father before the war:

NAME: Donald Harrison McElroy

DATE OF BIRTH: September 29, 1922

PLACE OF BIRTH: Sandwich, Ontario

NAMES OF PARENTS:

Garnet Andrew

Maude Elizabeth (née Harrison)

SIBLINGS: *(in birth order, and all younger than my father)*

Bernard

Joanne

Mary Ellen

PLACE OF RESIDENCE: 729 Riverside Drive, Windsor, Ontario

SCHOOLS: *(all in Windsor, Ontario)*

John McCrae School

Ontario Street School

Walkerville Collegiate Institute

RELIGIOUS DENOMINATION: Church of England

EYES: hazel

HAIR: medium brown

VISIBLE SCARS OR MARKS: scar on right index finger

He's about six feet in height, gangly, myopic, nearsighted, and wears glasses.

In The Box, this is what I have:

- a photograph he took of the Goodyear blimp at the Great Lakes Exposition in Cleveland in the late 1930s (*had*, actually, as I lost it in one of my many moves);
- a scan of a photograph from 1940 of a high-school basketball team on which he played;
- a sports patch, also from 1940, for soccer at Walkerville Collegiate Institute;
- a damaged hardback copy of *The Illustrated World History* (New York: Wm. H. Wise & Co., 1935) inscribed on the frontispiece "To Donald McElroy From Dad, Sept. 28 – '35."

That's it.

With no images of young Donald to make him real for me, he doesn't become flesh and blood until he's twenty-one.

2

CHAIN HOME

(TRIAD)

That's my father – the guy on the left. It's late 1943 or early 1944, and he's twenty-one-years old, a member of the Royal Canadian Air Force now for less than two years. He's been trained in a brand-new technology then called RDF (or radio direction finding) but which we now know as radar. He trained at one of the improbable centres of the technological universe circa 1940 – the small farming community of Clinton in southwestern Ontario – and here he is now, standing on the rocks of a place called Cape St. James, British Columbia, at a radar station located on the southern tip of the Queen Charlotte Islands. He's with a couple of his station mates and a dog. In a few months he'll be headed north, transferred to another station located at the northernmost tip of the island chain that makes up the Queen Charlottes.

~

But it's *this* place – Cape St. James – that he actually tries to tell me about some twenty-odd years later at our supper table in a rented home in the Pacific Northwest of the United States. He says something about how it had a railroad that ran almost vertically up the steep, rocky sides of the island, pulling supplies up to the radar site from a tiny seaside landing stage.

But I don't listen. I can't be more than ten years old. What does this have to do with me, with my world? With the typical self-absorption of a child, I decide that I'm not interested in such ancient history, and recommit my attention to the food on my plate.

And yet the fact is that I actually remember the moment of the telling. This incident stays in my mind still. Is it the story itself, or is it that my taciturn father actually told me something about his life? I like to think that it's both, but hey, let's be totally honest, here: this memory holds true because of the sheer novelty of an actual story from my father's past. Unlikeliness sticks.

But the picture: in it my father is leaning against the rock face slightly apart from the other two men, as if not really involved but just looking on. It's an appropriate image, an appropriate stance. It fits. From a man who never belonged, I too learned not to belong. Categorize this as amongst the lessons my father taught me.

It fits. Like a glove, maybe. Or maybe like a jail cell. Whatever the metaphor, it's all about one thing: exile – of the self-imposed variety. Well, maybe not totally. Me, I was always somewhat different: the new kid who started school after everyone else, the fat, clumsy kid who could be easily mocked, bullied and beaten up, the kid who had his milk money taken from him on a regular basis, who preferred reading to doing a lot of other things. I was a type, and there were (and still are) lots like me. Outsiders. Exiles.

Exile was imposed on me first. But then I chose it. Embraced it, really. Libraries became my safe haven. Books became my refuge. I hid in them both.

So all the me of the last couple of paragraphs is meant to lead up to this question: what exactly was it that my father hid behind – or from? Like him I've ended up always standing slightly apart, as if not really involved but just looking on. I know why I'm here the way I am (or at least I think I do), but just what happened to the child who was once my father that shaped him into the person I came to barely know – made him stand apart, I mean, made him opt for his own form of exile? Before these photographs that show him as a young air-force recruit plunked down at the edge of a continent to watch for a feared invasion by the Japanese military, there is nothing, save for a few undated snapshots of boats on his beloved Detroit River and the single photograph my sister Danielle actually possesses that shows him as part of his high-school basketball team.

There is nothing. I've never seen any snapshots of baby Donald, never encountered pictures of my adolescent father. Save for the discovery of the basketball team shot (in which my extremely near-sighted father isn't wearing glasses), I have no snapshots that show the gangly teenager he was. Growing up, I rarely saw his sisters Joanne and Mary Ellen, nor his brother Bernard – my aunts and uncle – and visits with my grandparents were never warm and fuzzy encounters replete with stories and anecdotes of young Donald. I heard no stories about my father from any of them. It's all a visual and anecdotal blank. For me, his only son, and for my three sisters, the person who becomes our father starts right here with a young man coming of age in the midst of World War II. Here is where something akin to an historical record begins, where the evidence of a life having been lived starts to accumulate via the photographs in The Box. Along with copies of the military service record, those photographs will track his life for the next few decades and ultimately tell me things about him I would never have otherwise known.

I can guess at some details, and possibly fill in some of the void. Like my father, his father, too, was an alcoholic. My younger sisters and I experienced it firsthand when we lived at my grandparents' home in the summer of 1967. We heard our grandfather's slurred impatience with us, saw him sit alone in the living room eating the lunch my grandmother set before him and drinking (skim milk laced with vodka) before he would head back to his architectural office in downtown Windsor for the remainder of the afternoon. Was he brutal to his eldest son, my father? I feared him as much as I did my own father, so I think it's a relatively safe bet to say probably yes. If it wasn't physical brutality, then it was most certainly of the emotional variety. And I would suspect that for my father, as for a lot of other young men of the time (like it was for my wife's father, growing up enduring the alcohol-fuelled abuse of *his* father), the military was a way out.

Salvation.

So this is what I know, courtesy the paper trail of his military record I obtain from the National Archives of Canada, and the photographs in The Box left me after his death: on July 2, 1942, just a few months shy of his twentieth birthday, salvation is at hand. He journeys from Windsor to Hamilton, Ontario, and there signs up for the Royal Canadian Air Force. His enlistment papers say he is a British subject and that he has signed on for the "duration of war."

Salvation is deferred temporary, for he's promptly sent home again. But six weeks later (and were they difficult weeks for him – did he tell his parents beforehand what he was going to do, were they furious with him over the die that had been cast, were they patriotically supportive, were they afraid? All of the above? Or none?), on August 16, he's recalled from "leave without pay" and the following day begins active service. After two months of basic training in Hamilton, he's transferred to No. 1 Manning Depot in Toronto – an enormous military clearing house located on the lakeshore grounds of the Canadian National Exhibition which housed hundreds, if not thousands, of new recruits at any one time – for further training and from there, on December 10, 1942, is sent to a place known as No. 31 Radio Direction Finding (RDF) School, Clinton.

You wouldn't know it now, but Clinton was one of the most important places in the world circa World War II. The only evidence these days of such status is an old postwar radar antenna and commemorative plaque that were set up on a small traffic island in the middle of town as a Centennial project in 1967. Not much, in other words, by way of honouring the fact that in 1942 when my father arrived, No. 31 RDF School, Clinton, was the only place in North America where you could be taught the then-new technology of what eventually came to be called radar. (*RA*dio *D*etection *A*nd *R*anging, "radar" was an acronym actually devised several years previous by S.M. Tucker and F.R. Furth, a couple of U.S. Navy officers, but which the British and Canadians would take a while to start using.) The school at Clinton opened in the late summer of 1941 and for the first couple of years was run by Britain's Royal Air Force. Three hundred members of the RAF had journeyed across the dangerous Atlantic to open the place and teach as part of the enormous and highly successful British Commonwealth Air Training Plan (BCATP). An international agreement made in the early months of World War II between Great Britain, Canada, Australia, and New Zealand, it brought young men from the far-flung corners of the British Empire primarily to learn to fly fighters and man bombers in the spacious and relatively safe skies of Canada. It became an RCAF–run school in July 1943, several months after my father had completed his training there. Actually situated in farm fields a mile or so outside the community of Clinton, it was a highly secure place complete with electrified fencing and armed guards. Students like my father were not even permitted to remove their lecture notes from secured areas lest the secrets of radar be possibly compromised. The powers-that-were had no intention of letting the radar genie out of its bottle. They wouldn't learn for a while that other genies in Japanese and German bottles existed (both countries had been individually developing their own radar technologies in the years before the war, though neither saw it as vitally an important technology as did the British and American militaries).

I rather suspect that, like most of his compatriots, learning the secrets of radar was not my father's first choice. Knowing his love of airplanes and flying (and for god's sake, I have pictures he took that are essentially photographs of clouds that reveal, only on inspection with a magnifying glass, tiny little images of airplanes flying about; and I still have a full-page newspaper clipping he saved – and later even carefully repaired with tape to preserve – from the January 3, 1941, issue of the *Detroit News* that shows images of "The Latest War Planes of Uncle Sam's Army and Navy"), I'm going to go out on a limb and say that when he joined the RCAF he really wanted to fly. His abysmal eyesight, however, would keep him grounded (and surely he must have known as much). So, quite by accident, he would end up becoming a bit of a pioneer – albeit a quite minor one – in the early years of a brand-new technology that would arguably win World War II, and play both an enormous role in giving shape to the postwar world as a whole, as well as the very course of my father's life from here on out. For better or worse, radar would leave its mark on him and eventually the family he would come to have. But this is all later. Right now it's all about adjusting to a new life on the cutting edge of new technology.

But all is not straightforwardly rosy. More than a quarter-century later he will submit an application to an employer in which he reveals that he began training at Clinton as a radar technician – someone who would mess about with the proverbial nuts and bolts of this complex technology to keep it working smoothly – but that training was ceased and instead he was trained as a radar operator. Nothing in his military records hints at this shift, and I would never have known about it save for this later transition in life from military to civilian and the fact that my father actually kept a copy of the application that, of course, now resides in The Box.

But no matter the mid-stream switch, here in wartime Canada, his life has absolutely everything to do with radar, another one of those technologies (and there are many) invented at different times by different people in different countries, some of which date back to the turn of the twentieth century. The version of consequence here was developed in England in the mid-1930s by Robert Watson Watt, a Scottish engineer working at the National Physical Laboratory in Teddington, England, with a background in the use of radio technology for weather research. He became involved in desperate, government-sanctioned research to develop a kind of "death ray" to be used against the pilots of enemy aircraft – specifically, those in German aircraft that the British government of the time knew would eventually be headed their way courtesy a newly militarized and highly aggressive Nazi regime. In the 1920s, the British Air Ministry even went so far as to offer a sizeable monetary prize to anyone – scientist or not – who could build the so-called death-ray device that could remotely kill a sheep from a hundred yards away.

The death-ray idea was a non-starter, but from it Watson Watt figured that pulses of transmitted radio waves could be bounced off objects and picked up by a receiver, and consequently be used to detect aircraft. He was right, and by the fall of 1939, the eastern and southern coastlines of England from the Orkney Islands off

Scotland in the north to the Isle of Wight in the south were swathed in a line of radar stations called Chain Home.

~

This system wasn't at all what we'd recognize today as radar. Usually the image that comes to mind is something rotating away inside a white geodesic dome and picking up objects that appear as blips on a screen. Chain Home didn't resemble that at all. Conventional radar today operates at extremely high radio frequencies on extremely short wavelengths – the microwave range of the radio spectrum – which means that a radar antenna can be small enough to be placed inside the relatively tight space of a protective cover like a geodesic dome. Watson Watt's first system, in contrast, operated on much lower frequencies and longer wavelengths because of the limitations of the vacuum tube–based electronics technology of the period, which meant that it required a vastly bigger antenna. The first Chain Home sites looked a lot like the transmitter sites of radio stations (and the first experimental stations actually tried to disguise themselves as such) with enormous towers supporting miles of wire that constituted the actual radar antennae that transmitted radio frequency signals and then picked up the energy reflected back by something like an aircraft or ship.

In August 1939, just weeks before the outbreak of the war, the German military, which was very suspicious of the purpose behind these enormous antenna arrays being constructed along the English coast, decided to investigate. They sent out an airship – the LZ-130 *Graf Zeppelin II*, an enormous hydrogen-filled dirigible – equipped with sophisticated sensing devices to cruise just barely off the British coastline and try and figure out what was going on. They were unsuccessful (they were probably listening for signals on the wrong frequencies), which was a great piece of luck for the British and would end up having enormous consequences for the war. Chain Home – and then a supplementary system called Chain Home Low, which utilized shorter wavelengths and consequently smaller, rotatable antennae to detect low-flying aircraft – would end up providing invaluable advance information of an attack by German aircraft. It offered just enough information to allow the British not to be caught off-guard and so be able to scramble squadrons of fighter aircraft to mount a defence in the air.

A lot happened in July 1940. The twenty-one Chain Home sites located along the eastern and southern coastline of England were put to the test in a very big way as what would come to be known as the Battle of Britain began. Here, on this side of the Atlantic, the Canadian government and military turned to the resources of the National Research Council to develop homegrown applications of radar technology. In that month – less than a year after war had been declared – Canada's first homegrown radar and the first in North America, a device called Night Watchman, was installed to protect the entrance to Halifax Harbour. To facilitate it all, a Crown corporation called Research Enterprises Limited was created to manufacture Canadian radar equipment.

For Canada, World War II was a mostly east–west war. Well, mostly east, what with the motherland under attack and marauding Nazi U-boats making the Atlantic Ocean a very dangerous place. To the west, the Axis power of Japan threatened, but in 1940 that war was still distant from Canadian water. *So far*. But it had occurred to the powers-that-be that ships and airplanes could provide only limited coastal protection for the country. The need of some kind of electronic defence of the long, unprotected Canadian coastline was becoming imperative, and the American military was nagging its Canadian counterpart to do something. So out on the West Coast, an early early-warning system of military personnel – No. 1 Coast Watch Unit, comprising small groups of men essentially equipped with little more than binoculars and radios to report whatever suspicious activity they might see – was set up in 1942. A stopgap measure, it set eight detachments at sites along the western shoreline of the Queen Charlotte Islands. But the continental edge needed radar, and as a Canadian system of Chain Home became a political and military priority, Research Enterprises Limited would produce homegrown versions of the British radar system, building 100 kilowatt transmitters and receivers that operated on a wavelength of 150 centimetres. (These were extremely long by today's microwave standards, but shorter than the original British system and comparable to their Chain Home Low system.) All of it, of course, was constrained and determined by vacuum-tube technology, which was unable to reliably produce much shorter-wavelength radiation in any kind of useful quantity. Eleven sites were established along the Pacific shoreline of British Columbia from the northern tip of the Queen Charlotte Islands to the southern tip of Vancouver Island, as well as thirty on the much more geographically complex Atlantic coastlines of Quebec, New Brunswick, Nova Scotia, Labrador, and the then-British colony of Newfoundland. RCAF personnel like my father manned them all.

And so via a circuitous route – from a beginning in Hamilton, Ontario, with important stops in southern Ontario at Clinton and Rockcliffe near Ottawa, where he attended No. 1 School of Flight Control – my father made his way, for the first time in his life, to the Pacific Coast. In June 1943 he arrives – equipped, amongst other things, with a roll-up canvas sewing kit (known as a "housewife") date-stamped for that year and which he hung on to through his entire life – at No. 3 Radio Unit, Vancouver, where he spends a little more than a week before moving on to his first Canadian Chain Home station, No. 13 Radio Unit at Amphitrite Point near Tofino on the western shore of Vancouver Island. It has the distinction of having been the very first Chain Home site constructed on the West Coast.

My father spends four months at Amphitrite Point, but I haven't a single identifiable photograph from his time here; maybe Don McElroy the avid amateur photographer put his camera aside while he adjusted to the demands of this new life of isolation at this seaside clearing in the woods, or maybe I just haven't been able to link as-yet-unidentified images lurking in The Box with this place. It isn't until he moves north in October that images – identifiable images – begin to appear, when he's transferred to Cape St. James on the southern tip of the Queen Charlotte Islands for a posting with No. 28 Radio Unit (radio call sign: "Triad"). He arrives on October 26, 1943 – two months to the day after construction of the station, then manned by one officer and three airmen, and sixteen days before the station becomes fully operational – delayed because heavy seas made impossible the shipboard landing (the only way on or off the island) from one of the converted fishing boats that supplied all the Chain Home sites on the Queen Charlottes.

All this coastal surveillance activity has to do with a spot off to the southwest in the middle of the Pacific Ocean called Pearl Harbor. Despite the U.S. request of the Canadian government to establish an electronic warning fence (i.e., radar) along the country's western perimeter to complement American efforts in Alaska and the Lower 48, the electronic defence of the coastline of British Columbia had only became truly urgent following the Japanese attack on the U.S.

View of Cape St. James vertical railway, barracks, and lighthouse

Pacific Fleet based at Pearl Harbor on the island of Oahu. After this attack on December 7, 1941, a possible threat to mainland North America began to seem a very real likelihood. (For the record, U.S. military radar sites on the island of Oahu had detected the incoming Japanese aircraft, but their information was disregarded and misinterpreted.) It was feared a successful invasion of the virtually uninhabited Queen Charlotte Islands – as the Japanese had done on some of the islands comprising Alaska's Aleutian chain – would create a staging point for attacks on mainland British Columbia, or that aircraft carriers would approach the mainland under cover of darkness and launch surprise attacks such as the one that had devastated Pearl Harbor. So in July 1942, orders were at last issued for the construction of the Chain Home radar system. Most were carved straight out of wilderness, and all were extremely remote and extremely difficult to access. Like Cape St. James. Comfort wasn't a priority ("no sign of Christmas turkeys which were hoped to be dropped in containers from plane," reads the December 23, 1943, entry in the daily diary kept by the commanding officer at the Cape); these stations were sited specifically to give their radar antennae unobstructed views of the ocean in specific directions. Each could cover a radius of about a hundred miles out to sea, and the entire chain was set up so that coverage areas overlapped. Tracks picked up by radar were communicated to filter rooms (on the Pacific Coast, they were located in Prince Rupert on the mainland and Victoria at the southern tip of Vancouver Island) where information was correlated and responses made as needed. It was Canada's very first line of electronic defence, and one of the very first in the world.

No. 28 Radio Unit, Cape St. James, was situated near a pre-existing lighthouse, maintained by a single keeper and his wife, located on the top of the hill more than three hundred feet above

View down vertical railway to landing platform at Cape St. James

the water. The Department of Transport apparently considered it rather useless because low cloud cover rendered it invisible much of the time, but it was found to be ideal for radar for which cloud cover wasn't a real problem. And so a station was created. At the shoreline was a small landing raft from which supplies and personnel could be brought in or sent out, and a cluster of buildings nearby: administration, recreation and mess halls, and a sick bay. Halfway up the steep slope was a small huddle of four barracks, and at the very top of the hill by the lighthouse was the radar station. All of it was connected by the long, extremely steep set of railroad tracks which I've seen described as an "aerial tramway" by which supplies could be hauled up or down the steep slopes of this place (and which were the only shred of a link I had for years to my father's past). The radar station itself wasn't much, just a single small building in which people like my father monitored activity at sea. Like other stations in the chain, it was rigged with dynamite to blow up the building and equipment so as to preserve the secrets of the radar technology should an enemy actually manage to get onto the island. It also featured a kind of large framework box holding the wire that was the actual radar antenna rotating atop a stubby wooden tower called a gantry. Information gathered was then relayed on to the filter centre in Prince Rupert.

My father spends four months at Cape St. James. The commanding officer's daily log details the difficulties of life in this place. Rations routinely ran low because the weather and rough seas made it impossible to offload from the vessel that supplied the station. Hunting and fishing helped supplement rations, and so deer and fish would regularly appear on the menu (October 18, 1943: "At 1030 hrs a deer was seen swimming from the nearest island to the southern point of this island. It came ashore there, and as the Detachment is

Langara Island domestic site

short of meat, was shot and prepared for the kitchen"). Powerful Pacific storms would blow down power lines and antennae, and play havoc with life (October 14, 1943: "wind reached great violence during night. Having great difficulty keeping doors on buildings and glass in doors. Forty-foot breakers seen on west side of island"). No supply of fresh water existed on the island, and so sea water was distilled (September 7, 1943: "RDF personnel succeeded in operating evaporators and producing a limited amount of distilled water. The only other water supply at present is that brought in steel drums from Rose Harbour, 17 miles distant. Lack of proper pumps makes regular operation of evaporators impossible"). The spray of salt water caused by storms often contaminated the fresh-water storage tanks.

Such difficulties were compounded by problems with the technology. Drive motors to rotate the radar antenna often broke down or powerful winds rendered it totally useless (November 2, 1943: "High winds make operations impossible at RDF site, aerial must be locked large part of time"). And even when the equipment functioned properly, the limitations of technology could show through (May 1, 1944: "Equipment operating satisfactorily but many spurious echoes on PPI [Plan Position Indicator, a cathode ray, television-like tube on which the radar signal reflecting back from an object would appear as a bright line] noted. Very difficult to distinguish between spurious echoes and echoes from aircraft").

Here's where my father's official military record seems to disagree with the on-the-ground realities of station diaries. The record says that he is transferred off of Cape St. James on February 7, arriving at his new posting the next day. But the station diary says differently, indicating that on February 19, 1944 (twelve years to the day, as it turns out, before my birth), he's one of three airmen

Langara Island radar operations site

transferred from Cape St. James who arrive at the station situated on the most northerly point of the Queen Charlotte chain (and the northernmost island on the Canadian West Coast), No. 26 Radio Unit, Langara Island.

There's a lighthouse here as well, maintained at the time by the Kinnear family – mom, dad, and two daughters – but in place of the monotonously rocky terrain of Cape St. James, there are trees – lots of them. And rather than a vertical railway track running up the rocky sides of a hill, there's a three-quarter-mile long road made of wooden planks. It traverses the rather more horizontal lay of land between the lighthouse and the radar station – itself established atop a small, flattened hilltop in a spot hastily cleared of trees that were left lying where they were cut – on this much larger piece of land.

And the photographs: my father was busy with his camera at both Cape St. James and Langara Island, and he's taken numerous shots. What I acquire just after his death is a jumble of black-and-white snapshots. But as I sort through The Box some order begins to appear. Images of the Chain Home sites are, for the most part, labelled as either being taken on the Cape or the Island; are denoted, in my father's neat printing, as "property of D.H. McElroy"; and are individually numbered. Only one – from Langara Island – is identified: a picture of another man on the back of which is written not his name but the place where the shot was taken, "Raff Bay," a spot on the leeward side of Langara Island.

There are gaps in the Cape and Island sequences where pictures have apparently gone missing, and I don't know how many pictures might have once comprised the numbered totals. And there are, too, numerous images that are unnumbered and unpropertied – photographic orphans of a sort. Two of them – both, I've managed to figure out, from Langara Island – depict my father. In one, he's

Don McElroy posing with friends in mock-execution scene

goofing around actually being one of the guys as the group goes about the task of cutting firewood. He rests his head on the wooden stairway that leads up to a barracks where laundry hangs on a line, waiting to have his head cut off by the other man in the picture who's wielding an axe.

The other photo is, like many of these images, poorly developed (likely an artifact of makeshift printing labs). It depicts a landscape of dense forest through which runs the double track of the Langara Island wooden road, three planks to each track, not quite straight and disappearing out of view at the distant vanishing point. Part of the way down the road stands a man. Though his face is indiscernible, I know it's my father just by the way he's standing. He's wearing a dark sweater – the same one he wears in the mock-execution scene – and light-coloured pants that, as he's in a pool of light filtering through the trees, and as the image was developed badly, overexposing this area of the print, they virtually blend in with the sun-lit wooden planks on which he stands. His hands are in his pockets, and he's looking back towards the camera.

Alone.

He's on Langara Island until the middle of November 1944 – an eight-month posting – when he's transferred again. He's back south again to Vancouver Island and to a posting with No. 33 Radio Unit, Tofino. Technology is changing; in 1940, before U.S. involvement in the war, the British reluctantly shared with them many of the secrets of radar they'd discovered. One of them – the big one, the one that would literally make all the difference in the world and arguably win the war for the Allies – was the cavity magnetron, a clever little piece of technology that produced very high-frequency, very short-wavelength energy that vacuum tubes could not. The cavity magnetron looked like a thick disk of solid metal through

Langara Island plank roadway with Don McElroy standing midway down

which a series of holes had been drilled and which were arranged in a concentric ring around, and connected to, a central hole. It could fit in the palm of your hand, it generated sizeable amounts of microwave energy, and it literally changed everything. This would be the direction radar would be developed; the lower-frequency, longer-wavelength technology of Chain Home was a temporary measure, and a technological dead end. The future lay with the microwaves.

No. 33 Radio Unit, Tofino, was a Microwave Early Warning (MEW) site, utilizing a transmitting and receiving frequency of 10.7 centimetres simply because that was the technology available. Magnetrons that produced electromagnetic radiation on such a short wavelength were being manufactured in Britain by the middle of 1942, and development of MEW technology in Canada began in July of that same year. It was hastened when German submarines boldly began to operate in the Gulf of St. Lawrence the following spring, and the first MEW sets were intended for anti-submarine warfare. But the possible threats from the air were not forgotten, and MEW sets specifically intended for detection of aircraft found themselves in places like Tofino. Technology was changing – fast – and my father, for the time being, was keeping pace with it.

The war ends for him in Tofino, where he's stationed through V-E Day in the spring and V-J Day in the summer until November 1945 (though according to his military record, he's on leave as of mid-October). Though a lighthouse in nearby Estevan had, according to some records, very likely been shelled by a Japanese submarine in June 1942, and though submarines were apparently spotted on occasion at various sites along the Pacific Coast (including off the Langara Island station on August 6, 1943, which reported "secret documents prepared for rapid destruction, demolition [of radar site] prepared"), my father's war was downright safe beyond the slight possibility of being blown to bits by an accidental discharge of the dynamite stashed beneath the radar operations building. No one actually tried to kill him, and hindsight makes it look cushy compared to what so many others endured: the nightmare of Canadian and British soldiers garrisoned in Hong Kong just as the Pacific war began in late 1941; the hell suffered by British, American, and Canadian troops coming ashore as part of the D-Day invasion of the Normandy coast of France; or the horrors experienced by American Marines at Iwo Jima and Guadalcanal in the Pacific ...

Using such comparisons, indeed my father's war was *very* cushy. But at the time, neither he nor anyone else stationed on the home front could have known this would be the case (though they may have hoped it to be so). The fact is that, while German U-boats prowled the East Coast for the longest time at will, torpedoing ships, dropping off spies, and even establishing a remote weather station in Labrador, the threat of Japanese invasion of the West Coast was deeply feared – so much so that the governments of both Canada and the United States turned upon their own citizens, incarcerating and seizing the property of citizens of Japanese ancestry in what was easily the most shameful aspect of the war on the home front. (Such racism was, of course, by no means new; in 1921 a woman named Hilda Glynn-Ward published a novel entitled *The Writing on the Wall* in which the Japanese set up secret air bases on the Queen Charlottes from which they launched deadly gas attacks on the major population centres of British Columbia.) The Japanese occupation of the islands of Kiska and Attu in the Aleutian archipelago off the Alaskan coastline in 1942 exaggerated fear amongst leaders and military planners in both the United States and Canada that the Queen Charlottes might be next in line and used as a springboard for attacks on mainland North America (though Japanese newsreel propaganda of the period shows the Aleutian Islands invasion as the first step of an attack directly on the city of San Francisco on the American mainland). The rising fear must have been quite tangible at the time for those like my father who spent their war keeping watch at isolated and lonely spots. As for the civilian population of a city like Vancouver, probably the closest they actually came to danger was from their own side when, in early December 1944, a disgruntled ex-RCAF flier who had been discharged several months earlier stole a B-25 Mitchell bomber and buzzed the city before crashing and killing himself near what is now Vancouver airport. (Reported in newspapers as far away as Australia, this was apparently a repeat performance of an unauthorized flight over Newfoundland in a much larger Liberator bomber that had led to his court martial and discharge.)

In the midst of all of this, did my father have any inkling at all that he would end up making a career of being a professional watcher? Was it inscribed in his genes, foreordained in his DNA? Or did upbringing and life experience make him thus? The prism through which I see him tells me of the fit of things, the appropriateness of the match between personality and profession. But I know it's a fit I force upon my historical father. It must be; the military powers simply needed people to do certain specific tasks. The obvious physical limitations of some may have narrowed the range of slots they could fill, but many slots were still available.

So surely my father came to radar – came to the field of professional watching – entirely by accident. They could have assigned him any number of other roles: cook, mechanic, file clerk ... Why this? Why professional watcher? Did some kind of military testing reveal the aptness of the fit? I have no answer; quite possibly he did show some aptitude for such things, but I've absolutely no evidence of that at all. And of this he typically never spoke.

The close of World War II ends his military adventure and his first experience of life (and maybe just a taste of a career) in the RCAF. He's discharged from active service on November 14, 1945, having earned, like so many others, a Canadian Volunteer Service Medal. He makes his way back to his parents' home in Windsor where (again like so many others) he'll finish up an education that had been put on hold during the war (or try to). He'll then take a path that will turn out to be a dead end and have consequences down the road: working towards becoming some small part of my grandfather's architectural practice. Willingly or not, the plan is that he's going to be getting into the family business.

It won't happen. But he doesn't know this as yet (though I think he may very well suspect it). For the time being, however, his days of watching professionally are over, and he becomes what he had been before the war.

A rank amateur.

3

YELLOW BEETLE

This is a Canso flying boat, the Canadian version of the American Consolidated PBY Catalina, an airplane that, like my father and so many other young men and women, came of age during World War II. In the photograph, a line runs from the stern of the aircraft to a mooring off camera, tying it up ashore. A truck is backed up in the water to the plane, and a man is pulling out supplies from its side cupola (where, during the war for which the airplane was designed, a machine gunner or observer would have sat). His buddies standing in the bed of the truck look towards the camera and smile. They're probably hollering at the cameraman. At my father.

On the back of the print, in my father's neat, draftsman-like handwriting, are the words "KITTIGAZUIT – How I arrived here." Of all his photographs in The Box, this is only one of a mere handful that has *any* kind of identifying information on it. This is it, this is the one: the photograph that goaded me into learning something – *anything* – about just who my father was and why this place meant something to him.

The airplane has RCAF markings on the fuselage; that information was someplace to start in figuring out what this picture – part of a number glued into a decaying old photo album that was in The Box – might be telling me. But the meaning of "Kittigazuit" eluded me.

Back up a bit.

The end of World War II saw my father demobilized – "demobbed," as the British might have put it; in November 1945, he left the military. According to his service record, he was transferred to the Reserve – "General Section, Class E," meaning he wasn't an active reserve member but available to be quickly pulled back into the military if a situation arose – and he returned to civilian life back in his hometown of Windsor. And again according to his military record, he attended night school in Detroit, listing his occupation as "architectural draftsman." Evening classes meant that while going to school he worked for his father as part of his architectural practice.

But first my father graduates high school. My sister Danielle comes across a copy of his Grade 13 "Upper School Examination" from 1947 at what was then called the Ontario Training and Re-Establishment Institute in Windsor, a place familiar to a lot of returning vets. She also comes up with his night school record from the College of Engineering of the Detroit Institute of Technology, which he enters ("As A Special Student," it notes) in early 1948. He scores a "B" in drawing, a "C" in algebra, and a "D" in report writing.

Summer 1948. My grandfather's architectural firm – G.A., McElroy, Architect – had just finished work on Dayus Stadium in Windsor, a twelve-hundred-seat outdoor facility for "Hard Ball – Soft Ball – Wrestling – Boxing – Midget Auto Racing" (as an advertisement in the *Windsor Star* phrased it at the time), which officially opened on Dominion Day that year. And he embarked on a renovation and building extension of the Kresge's store in Hamilton, one of a number he designed for the company when, between 1923 and 1950, he worked for the S.S. Kresge Company in Detroit as a staff architect while separately maintaining his Windsor office. (I consequently tend to think of my grandfather as having been a "five-and-dime" architect.) They're just a couple of projects his firm would've been at work on during the period that my father worked for him as a draftsman. Knowing the difficult relationship my father had with *his* father at the best of times, I can only guess that the strain of my grandfather's busy and demanding career put additional pressure on their relationship and that he undoubtedly wanted his eldest son to follow in his footsteps. And assuming (rightly I think) that alcohol would have figured into all of this on both their parts, it can't have been a happy time for my father.

Sure enough, late that summer, fewer than three years after he's left the military, he's back in again, re-enlisting in the RCAF – or, more accurately, transferring back into active military life from the Reserve. His papers list the date as September 13, 1948.

Salvation redux.

His service record lists him as a "radar operator." Immediately he's sent to RCAF Station Trenton for training to update his wartime skills. Located in southeastern Ontario to the west of Kingston on a site originally chosen for its proximity to both Ottawa and Toronto (as well as for the fact that it bordered on Lake Ontario, permitting sea planes to operate from there), Trenton is a place that is still very much an integral part of the Canadian military presence. Though the land for this site was purchased in 1929, the base didn't officially open as a Royal Canadian Air Force station until 1931. And like so many other bases across Canada, during World War II it became an important British Commonwealth Air Training Plan (BCATP) station, training fledgling pilots, radio operators, bomb aimers, and air gunners for the militaries of the Commonwealth countries who came to Canada to learn to fly or navigate or operate wireless, among other tasks. Early Cold War Trenton was a centre for transport airplanes flying as part of the Korean Airlift during the war there in the early 1950s, and a few years later was supposed to have become one of two headquarters for the continental air defence of North America (the other would have been in the United States, but the plan never came to fruition). It handles all the air operations – code-named "Operation Boxtop" – for Canadian Forces Station Alert on Ellesmere Island, the northernmost Canadian military post located only a few hundred miles from the North Pole. In the weeks following the attacks of 9/11, a couple of CF-18 interceptor jets were discreetly stationed here, sitting behind a fence, cockpit canopies open, on the ready, just in case. And Trenton was the centre of Canadian military involvement in Afghanistan: Hercules aircraft, enormous Globemaster transports (descendants of ones I would get to know intimately as a child and so which will consequently figure again later on in this story), and leased Russian heavy-lift cargo planes that carried troops and supplies to Afghanistan during Canadian involvement in the conflict there. The body of every returning soldier killed in that conflict arrived here first before taking the trip to Toronto along the section of Highway 401 that's come to be called the Highway of Heroes. People gathered at highway overpasses to honour the dead. Though I live just a mile away, I never went.

In 2000, my wife and I moved near Trenton, to the little village of Colborne (population two thousand) along the north shore of Lake Ontario that, when the wind blows out of the east, is sometimes beneath the flight path of incoming aircraft returning to the base. Trenton's just a short drive east along Highway 401, or a somewhat longer one along the old route, Highway 2, the primary highway through Colborne en route to or from Trenton in my father's day. He would've passed through, most likely via the train. It has absolutely nothing to do with why I ended up here – I didn't even know my father had once been stationed nearby until long after I moved here, the accidental histories of our lives seeming to cross even after his death. And sometimes, when the body of another soldier killed in Afghanistan was flown in and ceremoniously unloaded at Trenton, then grieved over by thousands of people who never knew him or her yet have some idea of the costs exacted by a distant war and so stood for hours in cold, rain, or heat on a highway overpass to acknowledge that price, I wondered if I would ever get out from under the military shadows first cast over my life by my father.

On a blustery winter's day several years ago, I drive east along the 401 just as an entourage heading from Trenton – police cars with flashing lights, a soldier's body in a hearse, and limousines full of family members – passed by in the westbound lanes en route to Toronto. The overpasses were shoulder to shoulder with people there to bear witness. On the far side of the highway I see an elderly vet – Legion beret and jacket flapping in the chilly wind, standing knee deep in the snow beside a highway on-ramp struggling to keep hold of a flag – and I lose it. I have to pull the car over onto the shoulder to stop and weep. It's not the dead soldier I cry for, nor that elderly vet with the flag facing down the elements, his own memories, and the known nearness of his own death. No, this is me remembering. This is me remembering my father staggering towards his own death, alcoholic, lungs tar-blackened from decades of cigarettes, dying of a toxic combination of Alzheimer's disease and prostate cancer. This is me remembering my mother's stories of growing up under Nazi military occupation and then Allied liberation in northeastern France near the city of Metz, and then, a little more than a decade later, leaving her family to follow her new husband to his next posting on another continent never to see her mother alive again. This is me remembering the emotional cost of what it was, as a child, to leave behind lives and relationships and a burgeoning sense of place and the first sense of belonging each time my family shuttled from one posting to the next; remembering my wife's stories of having to do the same as a military brat herself, and remembering my late mother-in-law, in whose house my wife and I now live and whose declining health was the reason we came here in the first place. A war bride, she followed her military husband from her urban home in Edinburgh, Scotland, after the end of World War II to find herself living rural amongst dirt-poor farmers and fishers on an isolated island in Lake Ontario near Kingston – her first Canadian home.

Because of an aging vet holding a flag on the side of a highway this is how I remember, unprepared for the vicious side-swipe of a rush of memories and knowledge I sometimes wish I didn't have, unprepared for the keen loss of people and times I wish I still did. You can call it the human condition, if you want, and think that I should learn to work my way through all of this. You'd be right, of course. Or you can call it self-pity, and think that I should just snap out of it. Right again. It doesn't matter, though. In the end it all boils down to the mundane fact that sometimes I really don't want to remember. Driving down Highway 401 is difficult enough without the weight of memory.

Here in Colborne, I – *we* – live in the shadows of flight paths. One is a constant: the path of commercial flights I only hear after they've passed overhead, passenger jets rising to the east from out of Pearson Airport in Toronto, fighting for altitude as they head off to Halifax or Europe. The other is military and occasional: the Trenton flight path with its transports flying low enough that sound and sight co-mingle, its use dependent on the day's wind and weather, or the imperatives of pilot training as Hercules transports or Airbus jets lift off from Trenton, circle, land, and repeat. Sometimes it feels like I've always lived under flight paths. I'm talking metaphor, here. For my father, who at first spent his time tracking aircraft second-hand on a radar screen and who would eventually spend so much of his life engaged with them first-hand, flying in and out of isolated postings (a large airplane, I learned from him, lands very differently on a short gravel runway than does a typical passenger jet at a typically busy commercial airport), flight paths were his everyday norm, his reality, his bread and butter. What I've known are the shadows they cast – the metaphors.

But I'm getting ahead of myself. Again.

On Valentine's Day, February 1949, my father is transferred from Trenton and heads off to his next posting, an air base near the small town of Gimli, Manitoba, on the shores of Lake Winnipeg, a place dear to the hearts of immigrant Icelanders who originally settled this place. Unlike Trenton, RCAF Station Gimli is part of the fading wallpaper of Canada's military past. The base was a product of World War II, when it sprang to military life as a part of the BCATP. Located there was No. 18 Service Flying Training School. And like so many of those other locations a part of the BCATP, that aspect of its life ceased with the end of the war. Gimli gamely hung on, though; in 1950, it was reactivated as a training base for the jet aircraft that replaced older propeller airplanes before finally closing for good in 1971. My father's presence there in 1948 falls in the transitional phase between the two rather distinct aspects of the station's life. But it had nothing to do with being a fighter control operator. His career has just taken a bit of a side road, for he's been posted to No. 2 LU.

LU is an acronym for Loran Unit, and Loran's yet another acronym: *LO*ng *RA*nge *N*avigation. It's a wartime technology, developed at the same place – becoming known in legend as the Rad Lab, a secretive U.S. military research facility at the Massachusetts Institute of Technology (MIT) in Cambridge, Massachusetts – where the invention that was radar was perfected during World War II into the useful wartime weapon that arguably defeated the Nazis, and where the atomic bomb got its start. Loran was the brainchild of a millionaire and amateur scientist who lived at a place improbably called Tuxedo Park, New York, and who claimed to have come up with the idea for it while taking a shower. His name was Alfred Lee Loomis, and, despite a Wall Street career that made him a fabulously wealthy man who could afford to build and staff his own private state-of-the-art laboratory near his home, he was no dilettante. Loomis was a scientific heavyweight, a pivotal figure in the wartime founding of the Rad Lab at MIT where the true potential of radar – in work begun in England – was developed into a variety of highly useful wartime technologies. His invention of Loran fell right in the middle of this fertile period, and was not without controversy.

Essentially the idea involved a network of transmitters – a master station bracketed by two so-called slave stations at opposite ends of the network – that synchronously transmitted pulsed radio waves. The signals formed a kind of grid, criss-crossing one another. A receiver in, say, an airplane or ship would receive these signals, note the discrepancies in the timing of different pulses, and use that information to determine its location. The idea worked great, and still does; until the advent of the network of satellites comprising the Global Positioning System (GPS), Loran was *the* navigation system of choice, with stations transmitting around the globe, and many today think the dismantling of the worldwide Loran system in favour of GPS is far too premature. (I've read of American commercial fisherman who used Loran to determine the locations of their lobster traps, and who found it to be far more precise than the only available version of GPS that the U.S. military, which oversees the satellite system, permitted to be used commercially until 2000.)

The controversy over Loran's invention arose because of its similarity to another system, devised by the British to assist their bombers in navigating to correct targets in Germany. It was called Gee, and British scientists revealed it to their American counterparts – Loomis amongst them – as part of a major sharing of information and technology (which included the revelation of the cavity magnetron) known as the Tizard Mission undertaken prior to direct U.S. involvement in the war. The morning after Loomis learned of Gee, he revealed his shower-inspired idea. Not everyone thought it to be a piece of original thinking.

No matter its origins, Loran worked, and it worked well, and its military application extended well beyond its use during World War II. Loran took my father to Gimli because Loran was about to become a tool in the Cold War. He's there training in its technology for a little more than six months, long enough to take part in the station's celebration of the twenty-fifth anniversary of the founding of the RCAF on April 1, 1949. More than a half-century later, I learn that it was important enough to him that he hung on to his souvenir copy of the menu from the celebratory dinner. That menu courteously provides a blank page for "Autographs" (he got none) opposite the menu listing (the main course served that night was "Filet Mignon with Mushroom Sauce" and formal toasts were offered to the King, the president of the United States, and, of course, the RCAF).

Through the spring and summer my father bumps around the Manitoba countryside as part of a small crew manning a mobile radiolocation truck, honing his Loran skills along the shores of

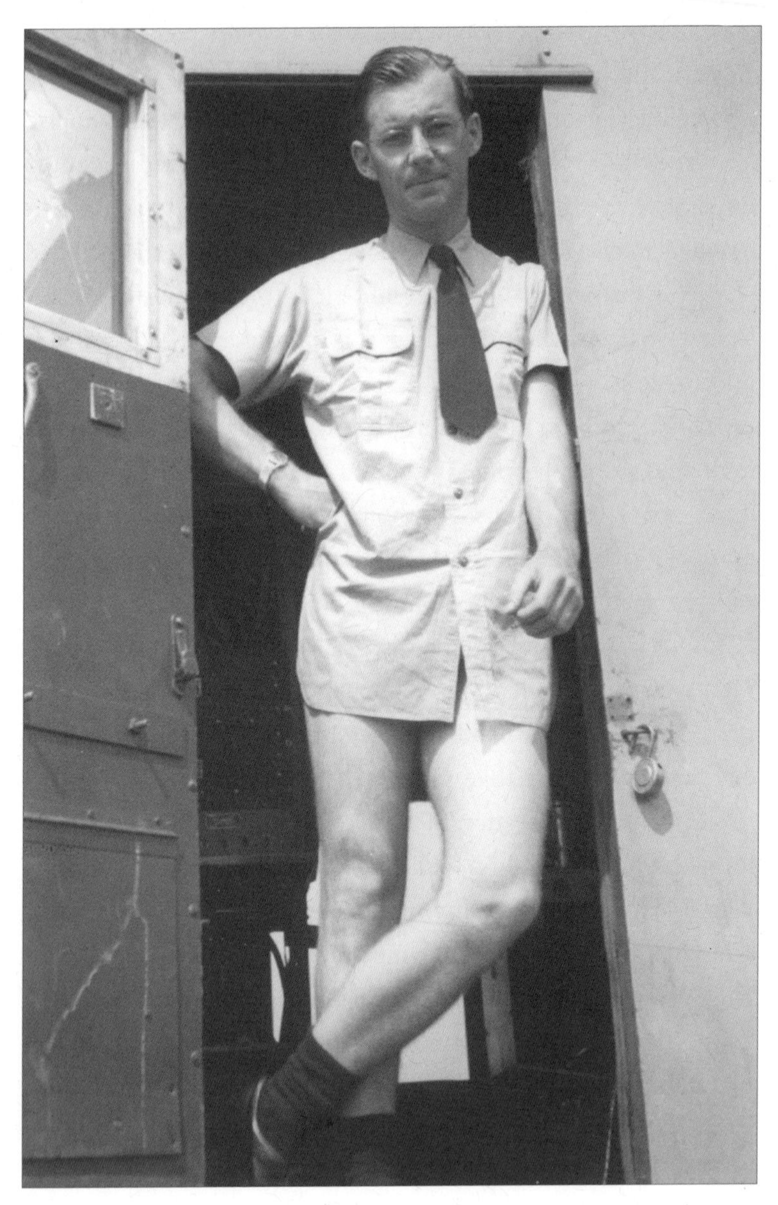

Don McElroy during training in Gimli, Manitoba

Lake Winnipeg. Someone photographs him with his camera looking less than pleased standing in the door of the truck dressed in regulation short-sleeve shirt and tie, but minus his presumably absconded pair of pants. On August 29, 1949, the same day the Soviets exploded *Pervaya Molniya,* or "First Lightning," their first atomic bomb (code-named "Joe 1" by the Americans, who learned of it five days later via one of a number of flights conducted by the United States meant to detect airborne radioactive dust) he arrives via Canso flying boat at the place for which, pants or not, he's just been trained: No. 4 LU, Kittigazuit, a place code-named "Yellow Beetle" located on the Mackenzie River Delta at the edge of the Beaufort Sea in the Northwest Territories. He won't know of this for a while, but with the explosion of a Soviet atomic bomb, the state of global affairs that's come to be called the Cold War has just entered a new, much more deadly, phase. The USAF and Great Britain's Royal Air Force have just spent more than a year flying supplies into the city of Berlin, then a city partially controlled by the Allies marooned deep in East Germany, that had its land route to West Germany blockaded by the Soviets the previous summer. And a month after my father's arrival in the Arctic, Chairman Mao Tse-Tung declares the formation of the People's Republic of China, posing what is seen in the United States – then at the height of the so-called Red Scare hysteria that saw the lives and livelihoods of many Americans destroyed in a veritable witch hunt against perceived communists – as a second major communist threat to the West.

Things are getting decidedly chillier.

~

Jimmy Doolittle is a name familiar to those of a certain generation.

On April 18, 1942, he led what became known as "The Doolittle Raid," in which American B-25 Mitchell bombers flew off of aircraft carriers in the Pacific to make the very first attack of World War II on the Japanese homeland. It accomplished little by way of causing actual physical damage, but made for terrific public relations and humiliated the Japanese military to the extent that it caused a shift in their decision-making that has been argued was consequential in the eventual defeat of Japanese forces. It was a one-way mission with the planes that survived their low-level bombing of Japanese targets continuing on to China where the crews – all volunteers – parachuted out of airplanes they had nowhere to land to be aided on the ground by the pro-Allied Chinese.

Almost overnight, Doolittle – for whom the raid was his only combat mission of the war before he went on to eventually command the Eighth Air Force fighting in Europe – became a folk hero. Spencer Tracy portrayed him in the wartime film that immortalized the mission, *Thirty Seconds Over Tokyo*.

I mention Doolittle because of something he did after the end of the war that ended up figuring into my father's many years in the Arctic that began with Yellow Beetle. In 1945, as my father, like the vast majority of other veterans, is returning to civilian life, Doolittle (by now a general) was in Washington, D.C., to take part in a U.S. Senate military affairs committee hearing about American military security. With the Axis powers now destroyed, the wartime alliance of convenience with the Soviet Union had come to an end, and concerns were rising that the greatest postwar threat to the United States would come from this burgeoning Stalinist superpower. And so Doolittle, to help drive that point home to the politicians who were scheduled to meet here, arranged that a map be put on the wall in this room where the hearings were being held. It wasn't your standard world map that depicted the globe in what's known as Mercator projection, the planet flattened out two-dimensionally so all the continents (their shapes and sizes distorted by the shortcomings of this system of mapping) and oceans appear laid out within a large rectangle. Instead, Doolittle deliberately chose a map that depicted polar projection – a map centred on the North Pole and which depicts a circle encompassing the land mass and oceans of the northern hemisphere. Doolittle arranged for that map to be displayed in the committee room so the enormous land mass of the Union of Soviet Socialist Republics was situated menacingly above that of the United States of America.

Doolittle was by no means the first person to point out the strategic importance of the Arctic, or to recognize that it posed a major weak spot in the defence of North America. Back in 1922, while checking out the possibilities of flying in the Arctic, Canadian Robert Logan prepared a report debated in the House of Commons stressing the relative ease with which an attack could be made by aircraft flying into North America from across the North Pole. There was, then, a growing sense that the Arctic would be the next battleground.

And so here's where Yellow Beetle comes into the picture. Operation Beetle, of which Yellow Beetle was the master station (slave stations were located at Skull Cliff, Alaska, to the west, and Cambridge Bay, Northwest Territories, to the east) comprised a secret chain of experimental Loran radio navigation stations established jointly by the newly minted U.S. Air Force (until September 1947, it had been the U.S. *Army* Air Force) and the RCAF in the Canadian Arctic in 1947. With the worry about a Soviet threat directly across the North Pole, the need to be able to move around – particularly, to fly airplanes – in the region became imperative for the militaries of the United States and Canada. But aerial navigation in the polar region is tricky. Something like a simple compass – anywhere else a highly useful piece of technology – doesn't work at all well when you're close to the magnetic pole, which yearly shifts its location. In the late twentieth century, GPS made it easy to locate oneself reasonably accurately no matter your location on the planet. (The American military kept the highly accurate version just for themselves until President Bill Clinton reversed that decision in 2000.) GPS is generated courtesy a series of satellites in orbit around the earth, but in the middle part of the century when satellites were the province of visionaries like the novelist Arthur C. Clarke (he of *2001: A Space Odyssey* fame), it was very different. Celestial navigation – using the stars to locate oneself – was one of only a couple of viable ways of getting around (which included the use of a device known as a directional gyroscope), but in the polar summer with round-the-clock daylight, it could be somewhat problematic. Enter Loran.

Operation Beetle used a system of LF – Low Frequency – Loran, which was different than typical Loran sites which work on higher-frequency radio wavelengths. It was believed at the time that low frequency, which can more easily cover great distances than its higher-frequency kin, was better suited to the enormous expanse of the Arctic. How radio waves were reflected between the two extremes of the earth and the planet's ionosphere – a region of the atmosphere that begins about thirty miles up and which comprises electrically charged atomic particles which are particularly good at reflecting radio-wave energy – was absolutely critical to the timing of how Loran pulses were received by an airplane navigating its way in the Arctic.

Gimli figures into all of this because experimentation with

LF Loran had begun immediately following the end of World War II when a test chain of such stations had been set up farther south in Canada with a master station located in North Battleford, Saskatchewan, and two slave stations in Dawson Creek, British Columbia, and Gimli, Manitoba. A number of specially equipped American military aircraft – including a B-29 bomber, the same kind of airplane used to drop the atomic bombs on Hiroshima and Nagasaki – conducted test flights across northern Canada and the Arctic. It was all successful enough that it meant that my father would spend six months at a small RCAF base on the shores of Lake Winnipeg preparing for what would turn out to be an equally long deployment to a tiny Loran site located at the edge of the Beaufort Sea, and of all of this he never – ever – spoke.

Wait. I'm running too fast, missing some important Canadian military history, here. The LF Loran chain of which Gimli was a part had importance to more than just the air forces of the United States and Canada. It was, in fact, an integral part of the overall militarization of the Arctic that began with Operation Musk Ox, a postwar three-thousand-mile scientific expedition from Churchill, Manitoba, to Edmonton, Alberta, via a route through the high north organized by the Canadian Army and that was meant to test the ability of ground units to get around in the polar region. Though the RCAF had embarked on an extensive campaign of aerial photography of the Arctic, maps of the polar region still weren't very detailed. The army decided that Loran would be exactly what Musk Ox needed to help it find its way, and so the chain of stations of which Gimli was a part became integral to this operation. It ended up with its own code name: "Musk Calf."

"Musk Calf." "Yellow Beetle." Add another name to the list: "The Roundel." The latter was thc official magazine published by the RCAF,

Don McElroy posing in front of a Quonset hut

and the August 1949 issue (the same month my father heads north) includes an article by Squadron Leader D. Gooderham entitled "So You're Going North?" It purports to offer, in a humorous way, advice on dealing with a posting to the Arctic. More specifically, it's about going to Yellow Beetle.

Will it be cold compared, say, with Winnipeg or Edmonton? Gooderham: "Here at Kittigazuit," he writes, "the lack of low temperatures has even been rather embarrassing," but, he cautions, "there have, indeed, been occasions when it has approached the frigidity it frequently attains at the corner of Portage and Main" in downtown Winnipeg.

What're the living quarters like? "Accommodation in general can best be described as satisfactory for the single man and, as almost everywhere else in Canada, inadequate for the married man."

How's the food? "It is difficult to write on the food question without sounding like a recruiting officer," he notes. "However, honesty requires me to state flatly that the food on the northern Unit is probably superior to that on the average southern Unit. On the Beetle Units it is superior to them all." My father, it seems, will at least eat well.

A sizeable number of images in The Box are from his posting to Yellow Beetle. A few of them even have something marginal to do with the food. On arrival in the late summer of 1949, he leaned against an oil barrel in front of a Quonset hut with his legs crossed and his hands in his pockets, attempting both a casual pose and a smile for the camera. On the day he departed on February 28, 1950 – three weeks after orders had been issued for the station's closure, days before all the U.S. military personnel posted there left, and a couple of weeks before the very last RCAF personnel departed – he stood in his parka and newly grown moustache on a runway cleared

Don McElroy operates an impedance bridge at Yellow Beetle, wearing headphones to detect a weak resistance reading

of snow on the frozen surface of the Mackenzie River waiting to board the airplane that will take him south again. Both pictures bracket the images of his life during this time.

He's clearly fascinated by the Loran tower, for instance, with numerous pictures of this 630-foot-high structure that, with its companion towers at other sites, would've been by a long shot the tallest structure in the Arctic region and among the tallest structures in Canada. And he's also clearly fascinated by the Inuvialuit people who lived in the area, with equally numerous photographs of the adults and children, including one of a small child delighting in a litter of newborn puppies. No matter his reason for being here, though, he's a tourist, and his pictures reflect that relationship with his environment. So, like the typical tourist posing in front of a tourist attraction like the Eiffel Tower in Paris, or the Parthenon in Rome, he poses in front of the local equivalent: the burned-out wreckage of a Canso flying boat that had crash-landed on the river in the summer of 1948 killing one person aboard. He holds a rifle and leans against the badly damaged cockpit, which has been torn away from the rest of the airplane. Companion pictures depict some of his buddies doing the same.

There are numerous photographs from Christmas 1949, showing the parties that took place in that period: an image of a multi-tiered cake made for Christmas dinner, for example; group photographs of the entire station personnel formally dressed in uniform for the occasion (my father standing typically alone behind even the back row of men); and numerous shots of the men drinking and talking. But mainly drinking. It's even possible, through a subset of this grouping of pictures, to trace the decay of an evening's celebratory occasion, as the mood descends from some form of propriety into what clearly becomes drunken revelry. Ah, youth.

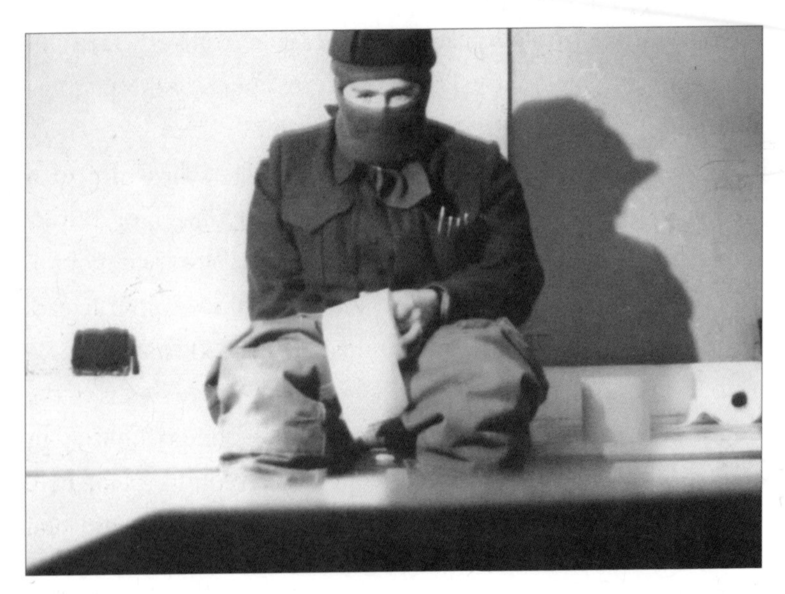

Washroom facilities at Yellow Beetle

There are photographs of life in the barracks, a series of landscape images showing the extent of the entire camp, and three separate "portraits" of individuals – hopefully friends, as these images wildly transgress the privacy line – sitting on the latrine, each with a roll of toilet paper in their hands, huddled against the cold in parkas and balaclavas, clearly freezing their literal and metaphorical asses off. A couple of other images show my father – moustached and headphoned – at work operating a piece of electronic equipment called an impedance bridge in one, and some unknown piece of equipment in another in which he holds the ends of pieces of string in each hand that lead off somewhere out of the shot. (I've had a number of former military personnel speculate on just what he's doing, and the leading theory is that he's trying to avoid being "bitten" by the build-up of an electrical charge on whatever piece of equipment he's controlling.) Still others show base personnel at their post, one operating what is in amateur radio circles called a bug – a high-speed Morse code key – used for base communications. (Though it seems anachronistic and slow now, Morse code was – and indeed, still is – reliable and could get messages through in difficult radio conditions because of the excellent discriminatory apparatus that is the human ear, which can detect meaningful signals amidst radio static.)

And then my father leaves. It's all been for naught; the project is a failure. Permafrost and ice have foiled the way low-frequency radio waves bounce between the earth and its ionosphere, and so the reception of pulses is highly inaccurate. Unable to pump enough electromagnetic energy into the system to overcome the effects of nature, the decision has been made by higher authorities to close the station. The last series of pictures from my father's posting to Yellow Beetle documents the arrival of an RCAF C-54 North Star aircraft

Runway on frozen Mackenzie River

on the winter ice runway, smoke from burning barrels marking the landing strip out for the aircraft.

It's the flight on which my father leaves Yellow Beetle. He stands for a last picture in front of the airplane's wing, moustached, hooded in a heavy winter parka, and with his uniform slung across one arm. Out in the wider world several countries (including Israel and Great Britain) have just recognized Mao Tse-Tung's Communist regime as the legitimate government of mainland China; U.S. President Harry Truman has just signed the country on for the development of the hydrogen bomb, which will make the atomic bombs dropped on Japan look like toys. Two weeks earlier, an enormous USAF Strategic Air Command B-36 bomber is forced to drop the unarmed atomic bomb it carried into the ocean somewhere off the coast of British Columbia before it then crashed in the provincial interior. (It will be the first, though by no means the last, such device the Americans would lose during the course of the Cold War, several of them in Canada.) And at about the same time, American Senator Joseph McCarthy is poised to begin the ugly process of rooting out supposed communists he claims have infiltrated the ranks of the State Department.

Through the lens of history, all of this forms a scenic, albeit highly selective, backdrop (though not, I suspect, much context) to the end of my father's experiences at Yellow Beetle and, indeed, the end of his involvement with Loran. The massive Loran tower will eventually be brought down, the problems with the Arctic application of the technology will eventually be sorted out, but he'll have nothing to do with any of it. He's been moved on to other responsibilities. It's been his first taste of the Arctic. In just under twenty years he'll be back.

But in the here and now of 1950, my father's been transferred

Don McElroy preparing to leave Yellow Beetle

to Canadian Joint Air Training Command in Rivers, Manitoba, another BCATP site west of Winnipeg and north of the city of Brandon. There he'll spend three weeks (and take a handful of touristy pictures: some military buddies, the town's train station, and the arriving steam locomotive that will take him farther south, which, like all good tourist pictures, reveal absolutely nothing about the parlous state of the world) before heading south, east, and back to Trenton for eight months.

Canadian political and military commitments to the Cold War will include involvement in the Korean conflict, but that won't directly affect my father. When he eventually leaves Canada for his first overseas posting, he will end up demonstrating to a group of stupefied Europeans that corn isn't just pig feed. Before that happens, though, he has to go home again.

Radar home.

4

SUGARCANE

(YELLOWJACK)

Of the nine hundred pages of my *Concise Oxford French Dictionary*, less than a page-and-a-half cover French words beginning with the letter "k". Most of them are actually of German, Serbian, Russian, Turkish, and Arabic origin, words that, over the course of time, have found themselves absorbed into the French lexicon. And of that bunch the bulk are German – as is "Kircher," my mother's maiden name.

I never knew when my parents' wedding anniversary was until March 2004, just after I had turned forty-eight years old. It was never something celebrated while I was a kid – at least, not something celebrated in the presence of my sisters and me – and as a typically self-involved child (not to mention teenager) it never even crossed my mind as something I might want to know or care about. I learned of the date only after I'd applied for and received copies of my father's military record. Innocuously buried in the documents were two dates: my parents' wedding and my birth. A thirteen-day gap separated the former from the latter.

Not much of a big deal – now. Back in 1956, it would have been more so, but we've not quite arrived there yet. At this point in the storytelling, we're still at the numerical tipping point of the twentieth century – 1950 – and the twenty-eight-year-old who would in a few years become my father (intentionally or not) has just left the

Arctic behind him for a while. He's been transferred to a familiar spot in southern Ontario.

In the course of trying to find out information about my father, I've managed to come across a number of photographs of him posted on various military-related websites (the picture above isn't one of them, so more about it later). The earliest of such images is one dated April 12, 1951. The day before – April 11 – is somewhat more significant historically, for it was on that day U.S. President Harry Truman decided he'd had enough of an egomaniacal four-star general who'd made a name for himself during World War II, and relieved General Douglas MacArthur of his position as head of U.S. forces battling North Korean and Chinese communist forces in Korea alongside United Nations troops from around the world (that included a sizeable contingent of Canadians).

It was a somewhat more newsworthy event than my father having his picture taken the following day along with a group of other young men, all of whom had come (or, like my father, come back) to Clinton, Ontario, for the express purpose of being instructors at the radar school located at the RCAF station there. He sits in the front row of the photo, second from the left, with sixteen other guys posed before blackboards in what appears to be a lecture theatre. He's still sporting the moustache he grew before leaving Yellow Beetle, and his pants are too short, showing us a little bit of bare ankle.

So my father has come home again. *Radar* home. He'd been posted to No. 1 Radar & Communication School (R&CS), Clinton, in November 1950 where he is set to work teaching fighter control operators (FCOs), and while still ranked as a lowly LAC, he is now a seasoned old hand teaching newbies the intricacies of electronic defence – more specifically, how to guide fighter aircraft to their targets. He'll be doing this for less than a year, until September 1951. In many respects, the way the military employs radar hasn't changed a great deal since World War II. Though it had long embraced the realm of microwaves, making possible that classic image of the rotating radar antenna which epitomizes the technology for so many of us, we're still talking about what is known as the "manual" era. This is the time period before the invention of the digital computer and its abilities to rapidly sift through and compare data changed everything. Instead, a radar site would, say, plot by hand on a map the direction and speed of a target that had been electronically detected until it passed out of the range of its radar and another station would then take over, all the while keeping a separate filter centre, which coordinated information, informed via telephone as to what was going on. Repeat as necessary. Sounds primitive and inefficient, and it was (though it had sufficed to guide British fighters to intercept incoming squadrons of Nazi bombers during the Battle of Britain and so arguably save the country from utter defeat early on during World War II). The situation was ripe for change, but that all shows up in another chapter.

So for ten months my father teaches what he knows at a station in southwestern Ontario set on the outskirts of the town of Clinton until, on September 15, 1951, just as the month-long Battle of Heartbreak Ridge begins in Korea, a fight which eventually claims the lives of almost 4,000 United Nations soldiers and more than 25,000 North Korean and Chinese, he's transferred to No. 1 Aircraft Control & Warning (AC&W) Unit at St. Hubert, Quebec.

There's some interesting history, here, for St. Hubert, on the southern side of the St. Lawrence River just outside Montreal, was built in the late 1920s, largely owing to the enthusiasm of then-Prime Minister William Lyon Mackenzie King, as a terminus for anticipated airship travel across the Atlantic from Great Britain expected to become part of a busy global transportation route (not an enthusiasm or belief, I must note, shared by all the countries comprising the British Empire of the time). In August 1930, it actually fulfilled that role – once – when the *R.100*, a brand-new passenger-carrying, hydrogen-filled British dirigible more than seven hundred feet in length, moored there following a seventy-nine-hour transatlantic crossing and turbulent passage down the St. Lawrence River valley that caused damage to the outer skin of the airship. (While they were by a long shot the biggest aircraft to fly our skies, and while they were constructed of tons of metal girders that gave them their rigid shape, dirigibles were in fact really quite fragile.) Coverage of the event in the media was enormous, and it's been estimated that more than a million people came to see the airship in the nine days it was moored at St. Hubert before the craft left on a flight that took it over Ottawa, Peterborough, Toronto, Niagara Falls, and back. The *R.100* returned to England just under two weeks after its arrival in Canada, never to return; the crash of its sister ship, the *R.101*, in France during an attempted flight to India two months after the *R.100*'s transatlantic crossing spelled the end of the British experience of airships. The *R.100* was broken up, its metal superstructure sold for scrap. The two-hundred-foot-high mooring mast built at St. Hubert would never be employed again, and in 1938 was dismantled.

But the airport lived on; it had been used for airmail services into northern Quebec from the time the place first opened in 1927, and until Dorval was constructed in the early years of World War II, it functioned as the main Montreal airport. During World War II itself, St. Hubert hosted a flying school that was part of the British Commonwealth Air Training Plan, and postwar squadrons of fighters and bombers were stationed there. It was just such aircraft that were of some consequence in my father's posting to St. Hubert. Of greater significance in Canadian military history (and to my father) was the fact that as of June 1951, a little more than three months before his transfer there, St. Hubert became home to the RCAF's Air Defence Command Headquarters, a function it fulfilled until that role was moved to North Bay, Ontario, in 1966 and St. Hubert's military significance gradually petered out. In 1996, it ended completely. The airport reinvented itself, and now functions as home to private flying schools that are a noisy irritant to nearby homeowners.

My father's posting at St. Hubert was brief – so brief as to possibly account for the fact that he takes no photographs while he's there. Yet it's a photographic blank that, viewed from this end of the historical lens, seems to me a wee bit odd in that the squadrons of fighters posted to the base – Sabre jets, brand-new at the time and the aircraft that distinguished itself in combat with Russian MIGs during the Korean War – would have been of *enormous* interest to my father, a true aficionado of military aircraft. I have numerous photographs he took at as-yet-undetermined air bases of parked aircraft (like a World War II–vintage Lancaster bomber, used by the RCAF in Canada for years in non-combat roles). So why no pictures of the Sabres?

In May 1952, he's transferred to No. 31 AC&W Unit located on the eastern edge of Toronto in Scarborough, and one month later is posted to the Air Defence Command Centre – No. 3 ADCC – that's been newly created there (though according to his service record, he isn't actually formally *transferred* to 3 ADCC until October 10, the same day he finally achieves the rank of corporal after four years of service). Situated on the Scarborough bluffs high over Lake

Ontario, the site had been built early in World War II as a radar-testing facility and then transformed into a radar school much like the one at Clinton. Following the end of the war the National Research Council continued to use it as an experimental testing site, sharing it with the RCAF which was providing defensive radar coverage of the city of Toronto from that location in a kind of ad hoc arrangement until a better system could be established. I've two images from that period I found in The Box, pictures that were quite likely taken by someone else (one of which has a woman's name and address written on the back in someone else's handwriting, the other with my father's notation of the station's three telephone numbers), showing my father – now sporting corporal's stripes on his jacket – playing bridge with three other airmen. But that's it. In any event, the posting to Scarborough is leading somewhere, for in June 1953 No. 3 ADCC is moved – along with my father – north to a spot just outside the city of Barrie, Ontario: RCAF Station Edgar.

Edgar (radio call sign: "Sugarcane") was part of the "something better" for providing Toronto with air defence, and this place on a hill to the northwest of the city of Barrie marks the beginning of my father's involvement with an entity known as the "Pinetree Line." It will figure in a bigger way later on in this story. In the meantime the short version is that the Pinetree Line comprised a line of radar sites constructed for the most part along the Canadian side of the forty-ninth parallel stretching from one side of the continent to the other and which was paid for (and largely manned for the first few years) by the American military by way of establishing an early warning and interceptor control system against possible attack by Soviet bombers flying from across the North Pole carrying nuclear bombs. RCAF Station Edgar is of consequence beyond my father's posting there: it has the double distinction of being the first of the

Pinetree Line sites established as well as being the most southerly of them all. Problems plagued its construction when work began in November 1950; a shortage of steel held up completion of the operations site where the radar domes were situated. While still not finished, it became operational in September 1952 (two months before the United States successfully detonated the first hydrogen bomb hundreds of times more powerful than the atomic bombs dropped on Japan and a dramatic upping of the stakes in the arms race developing between the U.S.S.R. and Western nations that includes Great Britain, which is a month away from successfully testing *its* first atomic weapon and consequently becoming the world's third nuclear power). Like other Pinetree Line sites, Edgar was designed to be family-friendly, and quarters for married personnel – called PMQs, short for Private Married Quarters – were made widely available, along with facilities that included a base school, and a recreation building that included a pool and gymnasium (RCAF standard issue for all Pinetree sites).

Not that "family-friendly" was yet an issue for my father. As a single airman, his life there would very likely have been that of the barracks and bar (and not necessarily, I think, in that order). The posting lasts for all of a month; in late July 1953, he gets a transfer that he'd very likely been hoping for: he's been posted overseas – specifically, to No. 1 Air Division Headquarters, a military base established in France as part of Canada's postwar commitment to NATO. It was situated in the historic walled city of Metz, a place that has a storied past. Located up in the northeastern corner of the country not far from the German border at a spot where the Moselle and Seille Rivers meet, it traces itself back to an ancient Celtic settlement that eventually became a Roman town. In more contemporary times it was fought over by the French and Germans, and became German territory in the late nineteenth century following the end of the Franco-Prussian War. After World War I, it again became, and has since remained, a part of France. This is where I'm from, the place where I was born, and what little I know of my Kircher ancestry suggests that this was when my maternal Germanic family became French.

My father's 1953 posting to Air Division Headquarters had him working out of the Chateau Mercy-les-Metz, a thirty-five-acre estate a few miles outside the city that still bore the wounds of World War II, during which the occupying Germans had used it as a military hospital. His transfer there happened just three months after the RCAF had moved its headquarters from Paris where it had been temporarily established in 1952. Canada's commitment to and involvement with NATO stems back to the organization's formation following the end of World War II. It comprised a mutual defence pact against possible Soviet aggression made between Canada and the United States on one side of the Atlantic pond, and Western European nations that initially included Belgium, Denmark, France, Iceland, Italy, Luxembourg, the Netherlands, Norway, Portugal, and the United Kingdom on the other. Canadian Air Division Headquarters remained at the chateau until 1967, when Charles de Gaulle unilaterally pulled France out of NATO. It was consequently relocated to Lahr, West Germany.

It wasn't exactly the lap of luxury that the idea of a French chateau might conjure up. That early on in the establishment of this Canadian overseas base, the few barracks built had been quickly filled to overflowing, so personnel were billeted in town. (Accommodations for families weren't completed until mid-1955.) The chateau itself was used for office space, and as central heating wasn't a concept whose time had yet arrived when the building was rebuilt in 1905 (for the third time in the history of the estate, which dates back to a Roman villa that had apparently existed on the site), in winter it was cold and damp. Out back, things were a bit different. Unlike home-front radar sites with their domes and comfortably contemporary operations buildings, 61 AC&W Squadron (call sign: "Yellowjack"), which by 1955 provided radar early warning detection of potential air threats from Soviet bloc nations over on the far side of what Winston Churchill had dubbed the Iron Curtain, and support for twelve fighter squadrons posted to the RCAF stations at Marville (1 Wing) and Grostenquin (2 Wing) in France, and Zweibrücken (3 Wing) and Baden-Soellingen (4 Wing) in West Germany, operated at a corner of the estate property out of ramshackle Quonset huts and had domeless radar antennae exposed to the elements that made the place look like a leftover from World War II. Inside the operations room, data picked up on radar scopes were then plotted manually by personnel using grease pencils to write on the back of large sheets of glass that held the mapped outline of the radar's range and which faced towards the radar operator consoles.

My father served, at least during part of his posting to Metz, with Crew 6, 61 AC&W. I know this minor fact only because in April 1956 he was photographed with his fellow crew members, one of nine men and an equal number of women whose job it was to monitor the airspace in this part of Europe. There were, of course, incidents that tested the fragile and tenuous peace that held through the Cold War. For instance, considerable anxiety was posed in early 1956 by the release in West Germany of weather balloons (a project reportedly nicknamed "Volleyball") ostensibly meant for meteorological purposes, and the daily log for this period kept by the commanding officer of 61 AC&W details both their releases and the consequential heightened state of alert in anticipation of possible responses from the other side of the Iron Curtain as the balloons inevitably drifted eastward. Later that year, flights by Soviet Tupolev Tu-104 passenger jets between Moscow and London sparked some interest and were closely monitored, but they paled in comparison with the first detection that summer of a flight by the then-new American U-2 spy plane developed by the Central Intelligence Agency and recently deployed in West Germany for secret, high-altitude flights penetrating the Iron Curtain to see and photograph just what the hell was going on behind it. Canadian fighters were scrambled to intercept the unknown interloper flying at some sixty thousand feet in altitude. According to the log entry for that day (June 16), once it was visually determined what the airplane was and that it was part of a highly classified project, the commanding officer ordered that future intercepts of such flights, too, would be classified. Other logs, however, do go on to note instances of detection of the aircraft as it headed out on missions to photograph Soviet military operations.

~

That's the historical background to my father's reason for being in Europe. As you've probably figured out by now, he never spoke of any of this. Doing what he did and being where he was, of course he would have been aware of things that were going on, and I wonder if he was working a shift when such incidents – flights of balloons, Russian passenger jets, American spy planes – happened. Probably so, but in any event he never spilled any of his secrets to me. What I have, in place of anything remotely anecdotal, in lieu of any stories from my father's lips about *anything* from this time period, are photographs, and so now this becomes a chapter about those pictures. The Box has a few things to say about it all.

Not surprisingly, Europe reignited my father's passion for the camera that from all available evidence – or lack of it – seemed to have settled into a period of dormancy following his tour of duty in the Canadian Arctic several years previous. His four-year posting to Metz results in an outpouring of images – both black-and-white prints and, for the first time, colour Kodachrome slides – as he explores the Old World. With no spouse or dependents yet to worry about, he uses his nondrinking income to buy himself a good camera (a German-made 35 mm Voigtländer Prominent), buy himself a car (a sporty red two-seater MG convertible), and sally forth across a good chunk of the continent with friends. The torn picture that my sister Danielle found and passed along to me and that heads up this part of the journey was taken somewhere along the way.

I didn't know just where it had been taken until I started closely examining his collection of colour slide images. Unlike his black-and-white print images, he kept these carefully organized in slide carousels that were individually dated and chronologically organized, and so form a narrative I can follow. These images – my father's very first forays into colour – begin in 1953 with a sequence of three images showing a military parade – through the streets of … Metz? The crowds on either side of the road are in coats, the background trees bare of leaves, as American troops march past. Then there are pictures of a different parade at a different time of year – the trees now in full bloom – and *then* the Grand Tour of Europe begins as my father sets to exploring the continent.

And there it is: the second slide image documenting this beginning of European exploration exactly matches the camera angle and landscape of that torn and bent black-and-white image in which my father stands on an unpaved French road, one hand in pocket, the other holding a camera, his double-breasted jacket open and

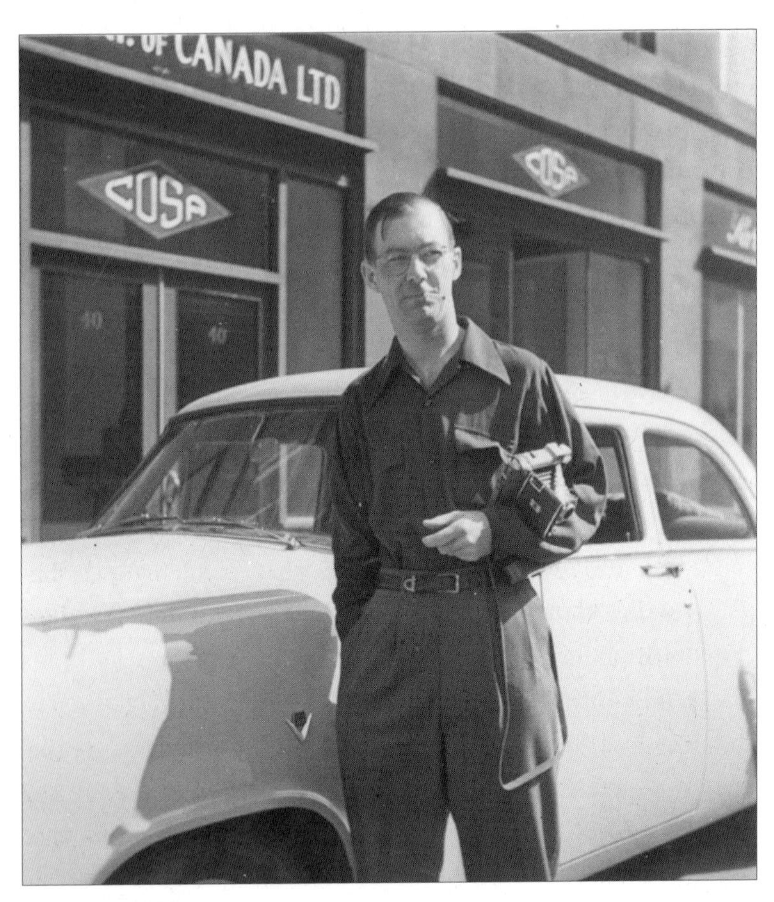

Don McElroy in Europe

a bit of foreground vehicle showing. In the slide duplicate of this scene, however, my father is nowhere to be seen. The image instead reveals more of the landscape of the distant and broad valley, and a nearby village dominated by the steeple of a church. Walking down the road leading to aforesaid valley and village there is a man who I'm sure isn't him. Still, I've a place to start.

Further along in the sequence are photographs he took while visiting the St. Mihiel American Cemetery, an enormous military burial ground where more than four thousand U.S. soldiers killed during World War I are interred. It's not far from Metz, so working backwards sequentially I'm assuming in the earlier image he's photographed standing on a country road not far from his French posting, from my mother's hometown, from what will in three years be the end of his bachelorhood and, thirteen days later, the place of my birth.

The clock is ticking.

The sombre images of neat, military rows of graveyard crosses are countered when my father's photographic gaze becomes truly that of the tourist. He and a friend with whom he's travelling and who he's photographed a couple of times make a stop to see the regal splendour of the palace and gardens of Versailles, and then enter Paris. The city provides my father with the requisite shots of the cathedral of Notre Dame, the Luxor Obelisk taken from Egypt in the 1830s and erected in the centre of the Place de la Concorde by King Louis Philippe, and many of the Eiffel Tower, into which images of my father's sports car are mixed (a couple of them show him sitting behind the wheel wearing a rather jaunty cap and dark glasses and looking really rather pleased with himself). And then there he is again, this time dressed in suit and tie, standing beside his car in Cannes on the French Riviera.

Don McElroy in Paris

The images take him on into Italy, where amidst the photographic conventions of tourism a pair of pictures offers up evidence that we can never escape our past. Among the collection are loads of the expected kinds of pictures, images of busy, ornamented classical architecture of engineering miscalculations like the Leaning Tower in Pisa, the much-more-successful Saint Peter's Basilica in Vatican City, the much-older Coliseum in Rome …

But then Don McElroy, son of an architect and trained draftsman, shows through: my father is clearly quite taken with the clean, Modernist elegance of the cantilevered roof and aluminum friezes of Rome's central train station, Roma Termini, completed only a few years before he saw it.

These are all a part of slide carousels my father labelled as having been taken between 1953 and 1955. They conclude with shots of the distant wintry Alps. Then things begin to get familial, for in the next carousel my mother appears for the first time. She's standing before the camera atop some old fortification which my father separately photographs in what is the last of his Kodachrome tourism, for the very next images are those of baby Gilbert in his mother's arms just before my father's tour of duty in Europe ends in 1957 and my father and his new family move back to North America.

Through all of his colour-filled European adventure he's not given up on black-and-white photography, for in The Box a plethora of such pictures abound, the bulk of which have nothing to do with photographing the tourist hot spots but are more personal in nature. They're images of him and his friends – Canadian military people also enjoying the relatively exotic pleasures of a European posting – travelling about and doing a lot of drinking (he even takes pictures of an evidentiary table full of empty bottles as if it were a still life). The photographs I have are tiny, contact prints made

Ernestine and Gilbert McElroy, summer of 1956

on narrow strips of paper, often with three images to a strip. More, there are pictures here that seem to have no colour equivalents at all. Like those of my father and his friends on a visit to England, a country that is utterly absent from his well-ordered collection of slides. Or pictures from a trip somewhere in West Germany to watch a car race. Or another trip to Paris, where he visits the Louvre and takes pictures of some of the exhibits and architecture, but is as equally taken with a parked truck on the street below his hotel room, photographing it repeatedly for some reason I haven't been able to determine. Or a few images related to the reason he's here, in Europe, in the first place: pictures of the chateau of Air Division Command Headquarters, and some depicting a few of his fellow airmen and women relaxing outside the barracks. Personal, yes, but familial, no. In not a single black-and-white print from this European time is there an image of my mother, let alone his European-born son.

And the friends who do populate many of these images, those who accompanied him – or whom he accompanied – to Paris, to a West German racetrack, or to a hotel room to share a few drinks, will disappear from my father's camera after this European experience comes to a close and he and his brand-new family are transferred to Canada (though in a world as small and closely knit as that of the RCAF, I know some of these people will be encountered again at some other posting, though never photographically). The stories these people fashioned together, too, will disappear, the threads of experience that bound them together in a particular place and at a particular time will unravel, their very existence hinted at only by images taken along the way but never fully and completely fleshed out within the limitations of the photographic frame. From my frustrated vantage point, the stories that bound these people together have died with them, for none were ever generationally passed along by my father.

And yet Metz has, for me, absolutely everything to do with these pictures, as few as there are. Perhaps even more importantly, Metz has absolutely everything to do with a critical *absence* of images. Amongst all of his photographs – slides or prints – not a single one shows my mother's family, and a total of only three of my mother on her home soil. And there is, of course, the void of silence that accompanies these images. The only stories I ever heard about my father's time in Europe never came from his lips. Only death unloosened some from my mother. Just after my father died and as she, my sisters, and I were sorting through some of his belongings, some stories began to come from her lips. Like how her family had sat agog at the supper table one evening watching as my father proceeded to boil up and eat corn from off the cob – what they knew as pig feed – right in front of them. Or how he apparently helped his mother-in-law get medical attention at a Canadian military hospital for her painful varicose veins.

On the maternal side of the familial equation, this is the set of facts that I know: my mother – Ernestine Amelie Justine Kircher – was born in October 1933 to father Maurice and mother Justine (née Staub). She is the eldest of eight children. She was six years old when France invaded Germany in the summer of 1940. As a child, she had her right index finger bitten off by one of the rabbits her family kept for food. They spent the war years under Nazi occupation until liberation by George Patton's troops in the November 1944 Battle of Metz. In my father's military record his father-in-law is listed as a "chauffeur," which, from what I've heard from my mother, meant that he was a truck driver.

Beyond that, there's just a smattering of stories, those few my mother has chosen to relate. And it is she who has preserved the only photographs of my maternal family I've ever seen. None of that came to my sisters or me via my father, and so of course I wonder about how that thirteen-day gap fits into all of this. How did this marriage all come about, and why the timing? Was my father pressured into doing the right thing by his outraged in-laws and/or commanding officer after getting a local girl pregnant? Or was it something like a problem getting permission from the military for him to marry that could account for the gap? In the papers I got from the National Archives, the authorization date listed for my parents' marriage is January 1, 1956, a little more than a month before it actually took place. Was this because of bureaucratic slowness on the part of Canadian authorities reluctant to give permission for one of their own to marry a local, or problems getting a reluctant groom to the altar? I know there's nothing remotely unique about my origins. But they are *my* origins, and so I of course ponder questions for which I have no answers. What I know really amounts to the fact that the winter of 1955–56 into which I was born was Europe's coldest in more than sixty years. That's about it.

In some larger sense, I suppose it really doesn't matter. The drama of my beginnings is synonymous with the drama of my parents' beginnings as a married couple, and so, I think, more rightly belongs to them and not me. And though I wonder about it all (a lot), I also sometimes think that in a weird way much of it is actually none of my business. My parents' marriage was their business, no one else's. They don't need to answer to me.

Or is this just self-serving cowardice on my part – an unwillingness to inquire into the perhaps less-than-pretty facts about a messy start in life? You're likely wondering why I haven't asked my mother about all of this, gotten the proverbial dope straight from the proverbial horse's mouth. At times I have indeed asked around the issue, and I'm not so totally oblivious to others not to have noticed the great discomfort and anxiety my questions induced in my mother, and to consequently have immediately backed off with my inquiries. Even I can see that this is stuff she doesn't want to talk about, information she is afraid to let go of, things doesn't want to expose deep emotions to the harsh light of day, memories she doesn't want to relive ... Like so many other families, mine is one that harbours secrets. And so that leaves this chasm of disparity, this yawning gap that spans far more than thirteen days between a wedding and a birth and separates my wanting to know from whence I came and why, and my *not wanting* to cause my mother more anguish than she's already known.

So I come back to what I have: the images. But the man who will shortly become my father photographed standing on some country road high above a French valley, or shown more formally sitting at a sergeant's mess dinner (having reached that rank in October 1954), or caught in snapshots standing with drink in hand in two other unrelated pictures can, when you come right down to it, tell me next to nothing about my past. Only the merest shards of his.

Maybe I've preferred it that way.

5

PINETREE

(MIDWIFE / REDTAPE)

SAXONIA
LIVERPOOL

In some ways, I'm a bit of an anachronistic throwback to another era, for I came to Canada an immigrant in the stereotypical way all immigrants once came to Canada: by boat.

Perhaps I should qualify that statement. I claim immigrant status when it suits me – when, say, it might impress someone or when it can prove useful in terms of getting someone's attention. Like now, for instance. But while it's technically factual (I held dual French-Canadian citizenship until I was twenty-one years old when I was required to choose between the two), it's a claim that, alas, I think has little actual truth to it, for being only seventeen months old – human baggage, essentially – I remember none of the experience. I think to honestly claim immigrant status you need to remember the process and all of its fears, uncertainties, and unknowings.

So my mother is the one who is the real immigrant, for she knew and felt its fears, experienced its uncertainties and unknowings. I need to acknowledge and honour that, for even as recently as 1957 when we came to Canada, immigration could still mean a cleavage from the family you left behind that could be final. It was so for my mother, for she would in fact never see her own mother again. Oh, there would be letters – many of them, written on thin onion-skin paper once ubiquitous for airmail delivery – and there was of course the telephone. But while transatlantic communication had existed since telegraph cables were first laid in the nineteenth century, and while telephone calls had been a reality (albeit, a mighty expensive one) since 1927 courtesy high-power radio links, the first telephone cable across the pond was only laid in 1956, the year I was born and a year before we came across. It was called TAT 1, and it offered the possibility of thirty-six calls being made simultaneously, each of which would have had to have been reserved ahead of time and with the length of time for the call predetermined. And it was still damn expensive (in 1956, a three-minute call between Montreal and London, England, for instance, cost twelve dollars) especially for a family living on a flight sergeant's salary, my father having attained that rank a few months before we sailed to what was, for my mother and me, the New World.

We departed on Wednesday, July 10, 1957, sailing Tourist Class aboard the Cunard liner RMS (Royal Mail Ship) *Saxonia*, leaving from Le Havre on the Normandy coast of France bound for Montreal with stops in Southampton, England, Cobh, Ireland, and Quebec City. There are, of course, photographs (slides, actually) my father took just before departure, like this one of my pregnant mother standing at the ship's railing, and another of her again at the rail but squatting down supporting a diapered me standing shakily upright on the deck. She looks off to one side, smiling at someone or something off-camera. I stare straight ahead, with serious and fearfully suspicious uncertainty, at the cameraman – at my father. No doubt I had no idea what the hell was going on, a look most who know me are quite familiar with still. There are no pictures of my maternal relatives amidst this subgroup of my father's photographs, nothing of us being seen off by my mother's kin. There is a familial void, here, one that starts at my birth and extends the length of my life. There is the utter absence of half my family.

No one waves goodbye.

But the voyage. My father saved a bunch of souvenirs from the trip. In The Box I have, for instance, a copy of the ship's "List of Passengers," many of whom were, like us, military people on their way back to Canada following completion of a European posting (like all other male children, I am listed as per the formal conventions of the time as "Master"; young women are all "Miss"). I have copies of all but one of the luncheon menus, a copy of the "Programme of Events" from July 11 (which tells me that we who boarded at Le Havre were requested by the captain to attend a boat drill that day "wearing Lifejackets"; that a radio news broadcast was held at six o'clock in the evening "reception conditions permitting"; and that the film *Twelve Angry Men* was screened twice that day), and, perhaps most oddly (and tellingly), paper cocktail coasters from the ship's bar where, according to my mother, my father spent a good deal of his time during the voyage. Also according to my mother I apparently had a great time in the ship's nursery while she lingered in sick bay enduring a double dose of pregnancy and seasickness.

The trip took a week, and upon disembarking in Montreal we climbed into my father's black four-door MG (the family vehicle for which he had traded in the sporty red convertible he'd so prized and which he'd explored Europe with during his posting), that had travelled with us in the hold of the *Saxonia*, and drove southwest through Ontario all the way to Windsor and the Riverside Drive home of my grandparents where my mother was at long last introduced to her in-laws.

Now, this can't have been a good time for anyone older than my utterly oblivious seventeen months. My mother couldn't have been anything but scared to death, and her less-than-perfect command of the English language, her general foreign-ness, undoubtedly didn't endear her to my WASP-ish grandparents. What little family lore I've heard holds that my grandmother was a member of a socially prominent Windsor family (a Harrison) and that my ambitious grandfather may or may not have pursued her as a favourable match for an up-and-coming young architect with a promising future ahead of him (or, as I've recently discovered when I found a copy of their marriage certificate online, it might have had something to do with my grandmother being five months pregnant with my father). That may be unfair and utterly untrue, but such is the gossip. Knowing practically next to nothing about them other than that, I have nothing else to go by save for later, also less-than-pleasant experiences of them at that same Riverside Drive home which have only ever served to confirm my less-than-cherished memories of these people. But this was my mother's first (experience of my grandparents, that is), and I know it wasn't pleasant for her in the least. So again: here she was, having left her family and all she'd known behind on the far side of an ocean, utterly immersed in a very different culture, facing her husband's judgmental family. As a non-Anglo-Saxon Roman Catholic without any social background who'd married into a locally prominent Church of England family, I gather from all available evidence that she was found unsuitable and simply not up to snuff. But I must note with some degree of satisfaction, here, that all my grandparents' children married outside the WASP-line (a Ukrainian, a Pole, and a Jew figure into my extended family, all spouses at one time of my father's siblings). It's a wonder my grandmother survived it.

In Windsor that first Canadian summer, my father did what he seemed to do best: he left. Alone. As in: without us. Not exactly one of his shining moments, but, hey, duty called. He had to report to his next posting and so left my mother and me alone with my grandparents (who couldn't have been any more thrilled by this state of affairs than my mother was). Ostensibly it was so that he could find us a place to live and then come retrieve us, but I can't believe that this was his only option; methinks he heard the siren song of the bottle calling him, and reverting to bachelorhood made it all so much easier to comply. So I wonder: did my mother see the beginnings of a pattern emerging here? Back in Windsor, I was making life more uncomfortable for her. My crying apparently disturbed my grandfather, and so my mother spent a great deal of time taking refuge with me in Windsor parks. I can't begin to imagine the level of her heartsickness; as an immigrant with a tenuous hold of the English language and culture in which she was immersed, and having been virtually abandoned by her husband, it can't have been anything but intense.

All of this – *all* of it – has to do with a line that ran east to west from one side of the continent to the other that I briefly mentioned earlier: that military entity called the Pinetree Line. The idea of electronically defending the homeland had been implemented first during World War II, and my father had been a bit player in that. But that effort had been directed at threats from the east and west: against marauding U-boats and any other potential German sea efforts from across the Atlantic to the east, and against a potential Japanese invasion to the west. The Pinetree Line, on the other hand, was all about perpendicular postwar relations – or the lack of them – with the U.S.S.R., for it was directed north against a potential Soviet bomber fleet carrying atomic (and eventually, nuclear) bombs across the Arctic to drop on the industrialized heartland of the United States.

Pinetree's origins lay of course in the end of World War II, when the Allied alliance of convenience ended and the United

States and the U.S.S.R. set their paths on a collision course – you know, that Jimmy Doolittle story I've already told. The tools and weapons of choice were all those wonderful technologies born at MIT's Rad Lab: the atomic bomb to threaten annihilation with (a military technology that, while it had its genesis at the Rad Lab, was actually developed into a working weapon out in the isolated privacy of a mesa in New Mexico known as Los Alamos), and good old radar to provide warning against. Continental defence would encompass earth, sea, and sky. U.S. Navy blimps – the largest ever made by the Goodyear Company – constituting Airborne Early Warning Squadron 1 went aloft to provide round-the-clock radar coverage off the New York and New Jersey shores. A series of large oil platforms housing radar domes – known as Texas Towers – were also established offshore of the U.S. East Coast until, in early 1961, a horrendous storm washed one away and took the lives of the twenty-eight men aboard, leading to the end of this project as a whole. And the "earth" part encompassed the electronic picket fence of Pinetree.

Though it was established on coast-to-coast Canadian soil and for the most part situated just north of the U.S. border, the American military paid for a damn good chunk of it. Work began on its construction just after a formal agreement was hammered out between the two countries in 1951. Plans were for thirty-three stations, and for the first few years the U.S. Air Force controlled and manned seventeen of them.

We continue to have this quaint notion of Canadian sovereignty that's hardly borne out by the facts. During World War II British Prime Minister Winston Churchill gave the U.S. rights to bases in Newfoundland, then still a British colony but one administered by Canada, and those bases existed well on past its entry into

Confederation in 1949. And during World War II, the U.S. Army established a series of radar stations across northern Ontario as well as at the locks at Sault Ste. Marie over concerns about possible Nazi incursion into the heart of the continent via Hudson and James Bays to the north and possible attacks on the Sault locks to cripple vital Great Lakes shipping (a concern that the Canadian government of the time apparently thought was a bit overwrought, but played along to keep our southern neighbours happy). As the Cold War got a good running start in the early 1950s, American-controlled Pinetree Line bases sprang to life on Canadian soil – at places like Beaverlodge, for instance, not far from the city of Grand Prairie in northeastern Alberta. There, a wooden sign at the side of a rural road displayed the image of a stylized maple leaf inset with, well, the image of a pine tree, all of it framed by the words "U.S. Air Force" written above, and "919th AC&W Squadron" down below. The 919th Aircraft Control and Warning Squadron, first formed in Washington State in 1952 and originally comprising a total of one officer and one airman, was created just for this assignment. According to the squadron's Historical Report for the period April 1 to June 30, 1952, preparations for their posting to the wilds of Canada included familiarizing "squadron personnel with the customs, history, courtesy's [*sic*], and environment of the Canadians and their country," and screening a film about survival in the Arctic (I guess they figured northern Alberta was close enough).

One numeral earlier and in still keeping with the theme of compromised sovereignty, Baldy Hughes Air Station, located near Prince George, British Columbia, was manned by the USAF's 918th AC&W Squadron from its opening in 1955 until it was finally handed over to the RCAF in 1963. And still a few more numerals to the left on the number line, the 915th AC&W Squadron formed in New

Hampshire in 1952 went on, the next year, to man the newly built and remote Pinetree site at Sioux Lookout in northwestern Ontario for years before it was put back into Canadian hands.

Get the picture?

West of Ontario, all the Pinetree stations were originally USAF. Out on the east coast, it was a bit different. Like at St. Margaret's (one of its radio call signs: "Midwife"), a small village in northeastern New Brunswick about midway between the towns of Chatham on the Miramichi River (a community that had been RCAF Station training fliers and air observers during World War II and, as of 1949, training jet pilots and even, for a few years, being the home base for the *Golden Hawks* aerobatics team before the military finally shut the base down in 1995) and Richibucto on the Northumberland Strait separating the mainland from Prince Edward Island. St. Margaret's was a village small enough that, by the early 1950s, electricity was still a recent innovation and the post office was still someone's living room. A mobile RCAF radar unit was stationed here in 1949 in support of the air activities at Chatham, and in the early 1950s construction began on an actual station. It came online as part of Pinetree in November 1953, home to 21 AC&W Squadron.

It was here that we entered the Pinetree Line in the summer of 1957, our first Canadian posting as a family. Fifty-some odd years later my mother still remembered our address at St. Margaret's: 3 Watson Watt, a two-storey PMQ. I remember nearly nothing of our time there; only the merest slivers of memory exist, and even those are, I think, questionable. I have, for instance, a remembrance of looking out of our kitchen door, out and across a marshy area behind our PMQ, and watching a man who is wading across its watery expanse. My mother tells me there was no such landscape behind our home, and yet I persist in linking this image – is it an actual memory? – with that place. I've got photographs from that time, evidentiary things that would, you would think, render the shard false – here I am in one, shirtless, holding a toy gun on a dusty base road; in another I stand outside our front door beside my mother and sister Elizabeth looking utterly angelic in my bow tie and sweater – and yet, the memory persists like a strong afterimage burned into my mind. What kind of sun must I have been staring at to leave this mark etched so deeply into my memory?

A few words about growing up on a military base – some colour commentary, if you will. "Cocoon" isn't, I suppose, an inappropriate term to broadly label what life was like (for me, anyway). All your friends are in the same boat: the children of someone doing something military. You have absolutely no other reason for being in this place than that. Friendships you might develop will be short, for you will both inevitably be transferred out to somewhere else. Sameness reigned; your home – your PMQ – is interchangeable with everyone else's. Aside from the recreation centre, which had a gymnasium and pool, not a whole hell of a lot else was found on a base, most of which were relatively isolated from any nearby civilian community. Food basics – bread, milk, eggs – could be had at the small store on base, but for anything else you had to travel off base and into a nearby community. Life was small and insular – not necessarily a bad thing for a child – but I would suspect it could've driven a lot of parents out of their minds. Especially wives and mothers who, on a military base, hadn't a whole lot made available to them (especially if you had language issues, like my mother), and who were what we would today call "stay-at-home-moms."

My mother's memories of the time include her first encounter with lobsters, left, she recalls, live and presumably quite unhappy about their plight in a bag hanging on the door of our PMQ by

Gilbert McElroy at St. Margaret's Pinetree Line station, circa 1960

some friendly French-speaking locals. Of my father's recollections of our time in St. Margaret's, he only ever shared one with me, and it doesn't involve the place at all. In October 1958, he was sent with two other base personnel on a two-week course to Santa Monica in California. That part I got from a copy of the station log from the time. What my father passed along to me was the remembrance of having attended a television taping of *The New Bob Cummings Show* (where he apparently even got to shake hands with the star himself, a passionate flier who had served in the U.S. military) and in The Box a number of slide images of a U.S. Navy warship he toured, a motel which I'm only guessing might have been where he stayed while on course (though being billeted in a military barracks would seem to make more sense, so quite possibly it had some other meaning), and what I again can only guess to be the exterior of some movie star's home in Beverly Hills.

What I also got from the St. Margaret's station logs of the period was that this was all a busy and stressful time. They report a constant stream of almost daily overflights by USAF B-29 bombers and nuclear-equipped Strategic Air Command B-47 and B-52 bombers heading north on training missions that would be tracked by people like my father who would have to respond to and deal with problems created by the intentional radar jamming they created by way of testing ground defence units. In September 1957, just a few short months after our arrival, a number of overflights by a Soviet Tu-104 twin-engine passenger jet between the U.S.S.R. and New York City were tracked with enormous interest at the station. RCAF Air Defence Command in St. Hubert even sent research people to the station to take part in monitoring the flights, and complete records of the flights were taken back to command headquarters for further analysis.

We stayed at St. Margaret's for three years until the early spring of 1960, and then my family – minus my father – entered into a second, much longer banishment to Windsor during which my memories really begin, where the accuracy of remembrance is true and distinct and consequently sometimes painful. But it will keep for the moment. I'll leapfrog over it and come back to sniff it over later. For now, let's pretend it's the summer solstice, 1961, and we've re-entered the Line, posted (the day after staff from the Soviet Embassy in Ottawa are taken on a tour of the place, and less than two months before the Berlin Wall was erected, literalizing for a lot of people the metaphor of the Iron Curtain) to RCAF Station Beaverbank in Nova Scotia (call sign: "Redtape"), a Pinetree Line station built in 1953 with – you guessed it – American dollars, though manned right from the start by RCAF personnel. In the days before an enormously complex military computer system connected all the proverbial radar dots of stations across the continent into a coordinated network, in an era when radar units were considered to be manual operations, sites like Beaverbank essentially functioned on their own. Its nearness to an important seaport like Halifax, to the Atlantic seaboard in general, then, made it an important place for providing electronic warning against what were then thought to be those vast fleets of Soviet bombers ready to sweep over Canada on their way to bomb America into oblivion. Beaverbank was, in essence, an electronic twentieth-century version of the Citadel that, in various forms, guarded Halifax Harbour through the eighteenth and nineteenth centuries and which is today apparently the most visited national site in Canada.

Beaverbank was where my family – now comprising three children what with the addition of my sisters Elizabeth and Danielle, both born during our posting at St. Margaret's – spent the Cuban

Missile Crisis, a tiny little nothing of a rural place about twenty-five miles to the north of Halifax. It's here where my memory becomes truly fixed, of substance and import and duration.

Actually, the posting didn't occur quite that straightforwardly; there was no room at the proverbial Beaverbank inn at the time of our transfer in the summer of 1961, and so we lived for a time in a small two-bedroom apartment in nearby Bedford awaiting a PMQ. The one we eventually got (which my mother tells me was filthy) was one-half (the right, as seen from the street) of a one-storey, three-bedroom unit with a crawl space accessible through a hatch in the floor near the back door where my mother kept the potatoes and to which I would be dispatched on what I found to be frightening missions to retrieve what she needed for supper. Like all the other PMQs on the base, it was situated along one of a series of tiers built on a hillside that rose up from a flatter area at the bottom where the base's main buildings were located – administration, men's and women's barracks, the school, etc. – up eventually to the radar domes a mile or so away at the very top. Our tier was part of an expansion of the base, and in the winter I could toboggan down the slope directly outside our back door and across what seemed to a child to be an immensely wide and treeless field before encountering the homes of the original development. The summertime tier was where I first developed my fascination with airplanes, one, I hasten to add, which never turned into a love of actually flying. One bright summer day I watched a formation of *Golden Hawks* Mark 5 Sabre jets – the RCAF's original version of today's *Snowbirds* aerobatics team – flash by very low over the base and its radar domes (in something similar to the unauthorized low-level flights over isolated radar installations that military people would come to call "dome" or "bubble checks") as the team, which by then was stationed in Trenton,

Ontario, took part in an air show at the Shearwater military base in nearby Dartmouth. I was utterly awed by the planes' brilliant colours glittering in the sunlight, their speed, and the phenomenal roar of jet engines passing close by overhead – noise that was more than just something I merely heard, but physically felt from my head right down to my tingling toes.

Beaverbank was where I first encountered and mastered the somewhat simpler technologies of Western life: sitting on the concrete steps out the back door of our house, also in the bright summer sunshine, laboriously and painstakingly putting into practice the abstract loops and whorls of motion required to tie my shoes all by myself, for instance. And upon first entering the educational system in Grade 1 (for I never experienced kindergarten) at David Hornell School on the base where we sang "God Save the Queen" every morning, assembled *en masse* before Her portrait hanging in the tiny auditorium, I encountered the complexities of infinity on the perpendicular: the numeral "8," actually, which I could only construct by carefully stacking two drawn circles one atop the other, utterly mystified by the seemingly baroque series of movements involved in the technique of rendering the number in a single motion on the school blackboard.

School in Beaverbank was where Santa Claus became a reality when, at Christmas 1962, I experience the immense thrill of being chosen to be one of his reindeers for his visit to our school, and consequently having to fashion an appropriate head from a paper bag for the event held in the auditorium before the entire school, and then on Christmas Eve, listening to the radio to the exciting information of the radar tracking of Santa's sleigh (wondering if my father was involved with that, though never daring to ask) and his escort of military jets. And it was where, shortly before our transfer out, I first encountered Valentine's Day and the misnomer "Giblet," a misspelling given me by someone else still in the throes of their initial encounter with the written language, but which would somehow follow me to the far side of the continent with our next posting.

And Beaverbank was where my childhood met the stresses of what went on in the adult world around us all. Here are my first encounters with fear and my cherished lifelong companion, anxiety. It was inescapable stuff, for Cold War culture was built upon these emotions; they were its very bread and butter. My father walked the mile-long road up the hill to the domes each day because of geopolitical fear and anxiety; this very place we called home was carved out of the Nova Scotia forest because of them; the Pinetree Line existed solely for their benefit.

The Cuban Missile Crisis in October 1962 when the United States and the Soviet Union seemed headed for a sure nuclear show-down over Russian missiles based on the island of Cuba maybe best sums it up. The transcriptions I've seen of the logs kept by the station's commanding officer give an official, if, as it turns out, slightly inverted version of events – that on October 24, the base, like all others in Canada and the United States, was put on "Defcon 3" (though in reality it happened the day previous, just after U.S. President John F. Kennedy appeared on television announcing a military blockade of Cuba); that food was stockpiled; that makeshift dormitories were established to keep personnel close at hand; that security checks were conducted every hour around the clock in the Operations building and that civilian personnel working on the base were subjected to increased scrutiny; that on October 28, the day after an American U-2 spy plane was shot down by a surface-to-air missile over Cuba, firearms were issued "to all officers and W[arrant] O[fficer]s," and the base put on "Defcon 5" …

It's a little misleading, for the "Defcon" system – short for "*Def*ence readiness *Con*dition" – comprises five levels, with Defcon 5 actually being the normal everyday readiness level, and Defcon 3 (which is the level the Canadian and U.S. militaries – save for the Strategic Air Command, which went up to Defcon 2 – reached during the Cuban Missile Crisis (and for the attacks of 9/11, for that matter) takes the readiness level to an above-normal status. Why were firearms issued when the readiness level had actually dropped, for on October 28 the Soviets, under tremendous international pressure, had actually backed down and agreed to remove their missiles from Cuba, thus defusing nuclear tensions?

Maybe it's a transcription error; maybe in the heat of the moment someone just flubbed it. But in any event, the October 28 entry is the last of it. There are no further references to the crisis. As far as the narrative record that is the station log of that period is concerned, it all passes. It's all over and done with, the record going on to accumulate once again entries of normal, day-to-day operations. No place in the commanding officer's tally gives voice to other realities.

Like fear.

I remember fear. No, that's not quite right. I remember terror. A six-year-old kid is attuned enough to know when something is wrong by the change in behaviour of the adults around them. I remember it like this: my father's absence, my mother's elevated anxiety, the displaced normalcy of the small world within which I lived. I have only the haziest remembrance of the facts of the matter – the news reports of Soviet missiles spotted in Cuba, the sea blockage of the island by U.S. warships, the political posturing by both Soviets and Americans, President John F. Kennedy's televised words to his nation (and by default, ours) ... But I remember clearly the sensations of what not-normal felt like as the grown-ups around me responded emotionally (for how could they not?) to the very real possibility of war and the inevitability of nuclear annihilation to which it would lead. And I remember, of all things, the base bowling alley, located in the basement of a building, and how in my memory it doubled as a bomb shelter.

But searching through the records of the base I find no evidence of any such place. There was, of course, a recreation building – standard issue as would be found on any RCAF station of the period, with a pool, gymnasium, a small confectionary store, and post office – but there is no mention of a bowling alley.

So this, then, is an unreliable memory, no matter the clarity that it has for me. It seems to bear no absolute fidelity to fact. I'm shaken by this, by the realization that something so consequential could be so mis-remembered, mis-represented, and so wonder now about my memory of the air raid siren. It's rising and falling wail, too, connects me inextricably to Beaverbank, to the same period of devastatingly intense brinksmanship that so very nearly cost us our existence. I can hear it still, feel the terror rise in my gorge as it did some eighteen years later when, asleep in my apartment which had no telephone or television, I woke to the familiar wail as the air raid siren sounded atop the post-office building in downtown North Bay (at the time, the important centre of yet another nuclear bull's eye), a block from where I lived. I threw on some clothing and ran down into the street and towards the art gallery where I then worked to use the telephone there, wondering as I ran why everyone else didn't seem to be responding like me, then frantically dialled a friend's number as a cold sweat poured off my face only to find out they knew of nothing happening of geopolitical consequence, and then learned much later that day that the siren was simply being tested.

Maybe the 1962 bowling alley wasn't real, but the fear and anxiety most certainly were. This is the gift Beaverbank left me. This is what the stupidity of Cold War geopolitics gave to me.

Or maybe it was the milkman.

Maybe it wasn't the game of nuclear chicken by which we were all held hostage. Maybe in fact my lifelong affair with anxiety began with a milkman. Well, that's partly true. It actually began with my mother, but the milkman has become inextricably woven into the fabric of my fear, for in my memory his knock on the door of our PMQ one morning signifies its origins. He was there to be paid for the deliveries of milk, eggs, and butter he'd made, but for some reason – perhaps lack of money (a reality on a military salary in which much went towards my father's consumption of alcohol), perhaps her inability to communicate clearly and easily in a language with which she still struggled, perhaps something entirely else – my mother didn't answer the door. Instead, we hid, quiet and out of sight.

And there are shards of memory of my drunken father. Just distant fearful flickers of darkness and noise and the not-normal, and a childhood habit I developed of crawling out of my bed and into a compartment with sliding doors in the bed's headboard – a place where I would by day store my pyjamas and comic books – and spending the night there, cocooned and safe. Decades later, when I encounter station logs in which I know my father is peripherally mentioned, I read them with my guts in a knot. I'm terrified that I will meet up with his alcoholism once again as it might have existed in official form, only to learn, instead and to my immense relief, that he had once reported a barking dog, and another time had been sent on a training course with a number of other personnel to Air Defence Headquarters in St. Hubert.

We lasted at Beaverbank less than two years. It's an odd length for a station posting, which would typically have been at least a year longer. My mother remembers our apparently early transfer out as having to do with my father's drinking, of his having lost his paycheque during a bender with some other military drunks, of her complaints to the base commander, of his decision to remove my father – remove us – from the scene of the crime, to move us on to another posting and presumably let my father be someone else's headache.

But the fact is, I simply don't know why we left in the late winter of 1963. The station logs – which could at times be so detailed as to include minutiae like my father's report of a loose dog – are unusually vague and insubstantial for that period of time, so I can't confirm my mother's version of events. The mundane reality may very well be that our transfer probably had to do with the fact that the station had been deemed redundant – would, in fact, be shut down at the end of May the following year – and so personnel were likely being gradually transferred out in anticipation of the end of operations.

What I do know with certainty and from the vantage point of hindsight is that as we left I had just turned seven. My father was forty-one and well into the throes of alcoholism. Beyond the slivers of a few bad memories of drunkenness, I only remember him from Beaverbank with any kind of sharp clarity at Christmas 1962. It's because of two pictures I still have, black-and-white snapshots of him and me together. He's dressed in his bathrobe with bed hair still askew, setting up the train set I got as a present that year. Though I remember it as being easily the most exciting thing

Christmas 1962 at

Beaverbank Pinetree Line station

that had happened to me till then, you wouldn't know that from looking at the pictures. I stand solemnly and hands-off next to the board on which the trains were set, desperately anxious to play with my gift but deeply afraid of doing anything that my father might even remotely interpret as challenging his control of the moment. I feared the repercussions, as in my six-year-old mind and for my six-year-old body, they could be immense, often involving his belt and my behind. I'm not trying to suggest that for my father the belt was the solution to every crisis imposed by his children, but that in moments of real anger and frustration it was what he would reach out for, likely just as *his* father had with him. The Cuban Missile Crisis and the milkman may have brought anxiety and fear, but my father's belt was a source of mundane, everyday terror.

That moment and those pictures of me hands-off before a Christmas train set sum up the relationship I would have with my father for the remainder of his life. Seven years from this image he will have left, and I will grow through adolescence and on into manhood having never spoken truth to his belt.

Never ever.

6

MID-CANADA

Interregnum.

That's the right word.

I opt for its third and fourth definitions in my *Shorter Oxford English Dictionary*: "a cessation or suspension of the usual ruling power;" and "a breach of continuity; an interval, pause, vacant space," for its place in my life has nothing to do with its usual definitions, those that orbit the papal politics of the Vatican.

Rather, this all has to do with the city of Windsor, on the Detroit River in southern Ontario, and with a military base called RCAF Station Great Whale River, on Hudson Bay in northwestern Quebec. This is about interregnum definition four: a breach of continuity, one that comprised a period in the lives of my family when we returned from Maritime Canada to southern Ontario to live, for a little more than a year, in Windsor during a gap between two other military postings: RCAF Station St. Margaret's, New Brunswick (1957–60), and RCAF Station Beaverbank, Nova Scotia (1961–63), both part of the family-friendly Pinetree Line. And it's about interregnum definition three: a suspension of the usual ruling power, one that occurred when my father left us, his family, to undertake a tour of duty at a fairly isolated military posting that was part of a line of specialized radar stations that laterally traversed the geographical middle of Canada and which was usually called the Mid-Canada Line though sometimes the McGill Fence, but which is, in any event, all but forgotten today. The two definitions, as I'm applying them to my family's life, overlap one another. They make for a perfect fit.

This was a time of a profound breach in our family – a period of dislocation and familial disruption that would have deep and long-lasting consequences for us. The Box isn't a huge help, here. It holds only a very small accumulation of pictures from this time period – the merest scattering of images, only a couple of which are of my father and one of which is a product of military public relations and nothing to do with his own photographic desire. The photograph here, though, is one of the more common fatherless ones, an image of my mom and me standing in front of our rented home in Windsor. The gate at the top of the stairs is for my younger sisters of whom there were then two, both born during our time at St. Margaret's. It was obviously taken in warmer months, but according to my father's military record his posting to the Mid-Canada Line meant that he was gone as of April 1960, not returning to us until the late spring of 1961. I've always figured that he took the picture, but I don't really know one way or the other, and I have absolutely no recollection of having posed for it. Maybe it was shot on his return. Maybe it was a warm spring. We're in the southernmost city in Canada, after all.

~

What I do remember of this time most strongly, though, are two things: sex, and my father's absence, his nonpresence after he relocated us to Windsor from our posting at St. Margaret's. Though the city was the home of my grandparents who occupied a large home on Riverside Drive with a great view of the Detroit River and Belle Island smack in the middle of it, we – my mother, sisters, and

I – lived some distance away in one-half of a duplex on Ouellette Avenue, one of the city's main thoroughfares, where the sex part eventually comes into the story.

This was not our first time in Windsor. Our summer arrival from France in 1957 en route, eventually, to St. Margaret's constituted the first of our stays there – albeit one that was relatively brief in duration – and I've already told you how well *that* went. I don't know whose decision it was that we would live somewhere other than my grandparents' home while we were in the city for our second experience of the place – or why we would live in my father's hometown at all, for that matter (maybe I've just answered my own question). I don't know who objected more: my grandparents wanting no part of sheltering their son's foreign wife and noisy children for any length of time, or my mother wanting no part of living under the same roof with her sniffy and judgmental in-laws. To be entirely fair, though, it would've been quite a burden for my grandparents to carry for an entire year. For whatever reason my father had brought us all the way back to Windsor (I can only guess that it *was* because of the hometown advantage, and so provided him with some sense of rootedness – lucky him), the choice of the house on Ouellete Avenue seems, with the hindsight that fifty years offers, to have been the saner decision.

By day my second-floor bedroom window in our old Victorian half-a-house looked out upon a busy downtown street, and at night the illuminated signage of the Red Cross building burning brightly directly across the street from us kept the darkness at bay in my room. Now the sex part comes into the story, for it was during this Windsor interregnum that I discovered the erotic lure of mermaids (though, at four years of age, I obviously couldn't understand or label what it was I was feeling) courtesy their appearance in what I seem to recall was probably a Superman comic book. Their blonde hair fell *just so* down their shoulders and demurely across their naked chest to reveal the merest hint of cleavage, and I remember intently scouring our tiny backyard for any evidence of these utterly compelling creatures, driven by something deeply primal and instinctive that I had absolutely no understanding of. But other nonsexual experiences happened in Windsor as well. I rode, for instance, in my first elevator, one in a medical arts building located a few doors down the street from where we lived (still standing, as was our house, when last I saw it in 2007). It was a manually operated thing that sickeningly bounced up and down as the operator sought to meet a floor at the level, a sensation which I'm sure is at the root of my fear of flying. And it was in Windsor that my father as an absence in my family became commingled with my first memory of disappointment, all because of Christmas. Sometime shortly before that great event, my mother brought home a stick horse – you know, a child's toy consisting of a broomstick with the head of a horse mounted at one end and some reins for tiny hands to hold that was once very popular. As I remember it, Santa apparently wanted me and my next-oldest sister (for the third, Danielle, was still too young) to give it a try. And we did, spending the evening taking turns galloping joyfully around the house from brightly lit living room through the darkness of the hallway, kitchen, and dining room and back again as my mother watched over us. But at Christmas, I remember no stick horse – had Santa been angry with us? And I remember, too, that my father wasn't there – was *he* angry with us? My mother spent Christmas 1960 – her fourth in Canada, her fourth apart from her family in France – alone with her three young children. This is the keen edge of my memory of this time in the lives of my family.

That aloneness of my father's familial absence (and possibly the source of my disappointment) had to do with his posting to the Mid-Canada Line. Unlike our previous postings at Pinetree Line stations where families could live (though not always did), the Mid-Canada Line didn't work like that. Actually, it didn't have a lot of people attached to it at all; it was designed, for the most part, to be unmanned. But my father was posted there in April 1960, to one of the few manned sites on an electronic line that spanned the continent from Hopedale, Labrador, in the east to Dawson Creek, British Columbia, in the west, running along the fifty-fifth parallel and about midway between the southerly Pinetree and northerly DEW Lines.

Conceived in the early 1950s as a secondary line of continental defence should some of those damn Soviet nuclear-equipped bombers manage to make their way through the DEW Line undetected by its radars, work on its construction didn't begin until 1956. Several years before, two RCAF and one Canadian Army tractor trains – essentially tracked vehicles pulling loads of supplies and people – had been dispatched out across the region where sites were intended to be established in order to assess the feasibility of access to the area by land. Not surprisingly it wasn't (feasible, that is, in a region comprised so largely of muskeg). The decision was made that airlift would be the only real way of doing all of this – of building the Line, I mean – in any kind of reasonable time period. The bulk of that ended up being done by the helicopters of the 108 Communications Flight, the RCAF's first flying unit equipped solely with rotary wing aircraft and which was formed for the express purpose of helping construct and maintain the Line.

The ninety sites and eight bases that eventually comprised the Line became operational in January 1958. It was all supposed to cost a hundred million dollars, but in the end cost two-and-half times as much and the lives of five workers as well. And it was rendered obsolescent within a few years and shut down beginning in 1964 (the western half of the Line ceased operation in January of that year, but the eastern half functioned until April 1965 apparently because of security concerns expressed by our southern neighbours worried about protecting what was back then still the industrial heartland of their country). Unlike the great lines that spanned the continent to its north and to its south, the Mid-Canada Line was an entirely Canadian creation, developed, built (by a consortium of Canadian telephone companies also contracted to run the technical side), operated, and paid for right at home.

Also unlike its southerly compatriot, the Mid-Canada Line worked differently. No rotating radar units were situated along it to scan the skies for aforesaid attacking bombers, but instead a series of towers – more than three hundred feet in height – were located at the ninety sites across the continent that utilized a form of radar known as Doppler, a technology in which a receiver would detect a transmitted signal's shifts of frequency caused by an object in motion through it, giving away information on said object's location, speed, and the direction in which it was moving. It's commonplace technology now, used in weather forecasting to track the movement in weather systems – we see it in use every day on television weather reports showing the development and course of storm fronts and the like. But back in the 1950s, it was cutting-edge technology. The idea was that anything passing through the space monitored by the radar towers – that is, those pesky Soviet bombers that keep cropping up in this story – would be caught up in this electronic net that stretched from one coast to the other. Trouble was that those lumbering, propeller-powered Soviet bombers never materialized (and in truth never existed in any great quantity), becoming, instead, the threat of faster jet aircraft and then the even faster, more efficient (and, eventually, real quantifiable threat) intercontinental ballistic missile, rendering all of this expensive technology totally useless. Some fifty-six years after it was shut down, the Mid-Canada Line could still make news: a 2011 article in the *Globe and Mail* detailed the toxic mess left behind, that still exists, and which had yet to be cleaned up.

My father took part in all of this – running operations at RCAF Station Great Whale River located at the edge of the river of the same name (in French it's *Grande rivière de la Baleine*) on the Quebec side of Hudson Bay, one of the eight manned sites on the Line – for a little more than a year before heading south again and being briefly posted for the second time in his career to RCAF Station Edgar, part of the Pinetree Line, outside the city of Barrie.

But back to the fifty-fifth.

Oddly, a month to the day before he left for Great Whale River in April 1960, and about a month before Francis Gary Powers's U-2 spy plane – the kind my father would've likely spotted and tracked occasionally on the radar scope during his posting to Metz – is shot down over the Soviet Union causing something of an international incident and great propaganda for the Soviets, he was confirmed into the Anglican Church of Canada. I have his confirmation card. He'd been baptized eight months after his birth, but not confirmed until he was thirty-eight years old, about twenty-five years beyond the norm. So why now? Why was this suddenly important for a man who I never knew as in any way religious? Did this have something to do with my mother's insistence, or (as my wife thinks) the pushiness of a military chaplain and the fact that my sisters and I were ourselves only baptized a couple of days after Christmas 1959 four months previous?

Such rituals were once considered far more important than they are now, but I still have trouble understanding its relevance and/or connection to his imminent posting. Maybe there isn't any – relevance *or* connection, I mean. Maybe it's simply one of those anomalies that happen which accidentally coincide with other events, leading us to forge a link that isn't real. And so maybe I have made/will make the same kind of mistake in the bigger picture, in me trying to figure out who my father was. Maybe some of the links I forge are totally bogus, the product of looking back and linking up events that happened synchronously but which are utterly unrelated – like mentioning Francis Gary Powers and a religious Anglican confirmation in the same sentence by way of providing some kind of global context to events in my father's life, but which all too easily could be read as an attempt to meaningfully link the two events together. That's the trouble with my working method, I guess. Mistakes will happen, things will be misinterpreted, meanings made out of what essentially amounts to nothing at all. But I really don't have much to go on beyond the contextualizing historical knowledge of the events of the times in which my father lived. Just the official paper trail (or some of it, anyway) detailing my father's career, and a pile of pictures he took along the way. I have to put some kind of trust in them. I have to believe in The Box.

Deflatingly perhaps, it proffers merely the two pictures of my father from this time period. As I mentioned before, one of them isn't even familial. It's not a snapshot, and it's not an image he took himself; it has, instead, officialdom written all over it. It's an RCAF photograph – standard issue kind of thing that I think pretty much every serviceman or woman must've posed for at some point in their career – showing him sitting at a desk in uniform talking on the telephone and looking very serious and responsible. It ended up being reproduced in a Windsor newspaper (exact date unknown). I've a copy of the clipping. It's captioned thusly:

> RIVERSIDE AIRMAN AT GREAT WHALE RIVER – Flight Sergeant D.H. (Mac) McElroy of Riverside, Ont. is shown at his desk at the Mid Canada Line aircraft detection station at Great Whale River. Flight Sergeant McElroy, who joined the FCAF [*sic*] as a Fighter Control Operator in 1948, is the son of Mrs. G. A. McElroy of 729 Riverside Drive, Riverside.

Well, I really rather think I can trust my interpretation of things, here. To start with, notice that my mother – D.H. (Mac) McElroy's *spouse* – isn't mentioned at all. Just my grandmother. Her hand in all of this is loudly evident. If her daughters' weddings made the society page (I even have yellowed newspaper clippings announcing them and detailing who wore what that I found stuffed between pages of our family bible), I will make an educated leap towards the conclusion that she decided her first-born son was damn well going to show up somewhere in the paper (other than, say, in something equivalent to police reports or the obituaries) as someone of note. He would be Someone Worthy, or, perhaps even more importantly for my grandmother, Son of Someone Worthy. But not, apparently, Someone Married With Three Children.

Interestingly as well, my father, the keen photographer, apparently takes only two pictures during his time on the Quebec shore of Hudson Bay (maybe there were others, but The Box proffers only photographic certainties), one of which is a self-portrait standing in the snow, the other his commanding officer doing the same. That's it; The Box is otherwise photographically mute about this place. It's

Official RCAF photo of Don McElroy at Great Whale River

another of several odd visual silences from his military life – an unusual photographic gap within his absence from his family that can't have much to do with any formal military prohibitions against taking pictures (for many such images were taken). Such a void I do have difficulty interpreting. The only other pictures show more southerly subjects: a small flurry of family photos he presumably takes before his departure, and then the void begins during which there is nothing other than a few snapshots my mother takes of her children playing at Jackson Park up the street from our Windsor home in the hot summer of 1960. And then of course the image of my mother and me that could've been taken on my father's return.

So aside from the staged military photograph, a meagre handful of snapshots, and the newspaper clipping which I'm assuming proved itself useful to my society-conscious grandmother, the only other artifact I have from this time and place in my father's military life is a printed menu – RCAF logo on the cover – for Christmas dinner, 1960, at Great Whale River. Aside from the Commanding Officer, my father is the other senior RCAF person on the base (he's the "chief op[eration]s officer"), their names heading up the menu's printed list of the station personnel which included a large number of Canadian Marconi employees, and single representatives from each of Consolidated Engines Ltd., Spartan Air Services, and Crawley & McCracken Co. Ltd., all employees of companies involved in the operation of the Line. Autographs on the back cover, starting with "McElroy – THE IDIOT," show the signatures of many of the personnel on the printed list including, to my enormous surprise, the family members – wife and kids – of the commanding officer. (Almost fifty years later, I will learn to my astonishment that, because of his advanced age of thirty-five and the care and concern he shows them, he is affectionately called Dad by the younger RCAF personnel on the base.)

When he came back a year or so later (his return, like his departure, was an event I have no memory of), his lengthy absenteeism from his family would be acknowledged – commemorated? – with a plaque on the wall of one of the many homes in which we'd later live. It was made of wood, shield-shaped, and not all that big. On it was depicted a spouting white whale. This was my father's memento of Great Whale River; it hung on the walls of many homes for many years. And I've lost it.

I've lost the first souvenir my family had of my father's absence. I've lost the marker of a parental void – not my first (void that is), but the first one of which I have a memory. So here's what I consequently want to know: how do we remember and acknowledge absence in our lives? How do we remember the first removal, acknowledge the first void where someone important in our lives had been but is no longer? I would hazard a guess that for most of us it has little to do with things like wooden plaques and everything to do with the death of a family member – immediate or otherwise. But it wasn't that way for me. On the far side of that damn plaque is a stick horse, its presence and then its absence at the right time, felt enough for the memory to last, to stick hard and fast, remaining firm and true in my mind more than a half-century later. And while I remember my father's absence, it isn't an absence I keenly felt in the form of loss. What does this say about me?

I would again hazard a guess and say that I don't think it says much at all. It speaks more to the mind of a four-year-old, of the priorities of a four-year-old, of the fact that a stick horse gave more pleasure, more comfort than my father who, like I would think most men of his generation, remained at a psychological and emotional distance from his children, leaving the child-rearing and all its emotional and psychological shaping to women, to their wives. So the four-year-old me remembers my mother, her presence, her love, her caring, though not, of course, the anguish that must have been hers at having been left behind by her husband again, and in a place with no familiar faces excepting judgmental in-laws close at hand. My anguish was that of a stick horse never become mine, and not that of having been abandoned by my father. His absence never registered in any emotionally or psychologically significant way. I mean, I was aware of him not being there, but not in any bothersome way – not as a painful absence. Not as a loss.

Why is this important? I mean, I know why it has significance for *me*, as it formally denoted my first memory of my family as a group not including my father. But why does it matter in some bigger picture? Or *does* it matter at all in said bigger picture? Such a cleaving of the family unit is all intertwined within what, with the hindsight that the passage of time has offered, I think were great big whopping lies that were fed to us by the powers-that-were of the period, lies which were supposed to be believed and taken culturally to heart, (mis)shaping us and our consequent relationships with the world – with each other, I mean. I was of course far too young to know the subtleties of any of it. But out there beyond my limited sphere of reference, beyond the tiny backyard of our home that I scoured for imaginary mermaids, the lies – political, social, cultural – persisted and flourished. As I grew into manhood, I eventually came to know them.

This, then, is what I think is the real stick-horse story. We were, this version of the story would go, supposed to believe that this thing for which our fathers left us and that we called the Cold War was about the protection of a specific way of life, the preservation of certain values and freedoms that were not shared or even presumably dreamt of by our enemies on the far side of the Pole who apparently sought nothing more than our destruction. Or perhaps I should do the *Jeopardy!* thing and phrase it in the form of a question: *were* we to believe that this particular (for me and my sisters, fatherless) structure of our lives we called the Cold War was about the protection of a way of life and certain values from enemies out to do us in? Certainly popular culture would have us think so. In the 1955 film *Strategic Air Command*, Jimmy Stewart portrays a professional baseball player who is convinced so and gives up his career to do the Right Thing and return to the military in which he had once served, and to again defend his country and the American Way of Life flying B-36 bombers, the largest ever built by the USAF and which were intended solely to carry atomic and nuclear weaponry by way of retaliation for a Soviet first strike. (To be fair to the filmic plot line, by the end of the movie Stewart, having done His Duty and even been injured in the process in a plane crash in Greenland, does leave the military again and make a return to baseball.) Or the 1963 film *A Gathering of Eagles*, which has Rock Hudson playing a hard-assed Strategic Air Command base commander driving his men (and by consequence their families) to the edge of personal and familial breakdown as he shapes them up to be the perfect counterstrike force (this time flying the B-52 bombers that replaced the B-36, airplanes that are today still the mainstay of the USAF bombing fleet) for a Soviet attack on Western Values – by which I mean, of course, the United States of America.

Were these films pure propaganda or did most of their audiences take part in a more culturally *laissez-faire* attitude towards the Cold War and the threat of nuclear annihilation? Did the Cold War really figure in any significant way in how we (and I mean by that pronoun North American society in general) went about our everyday lives? Or did we, instead, just try to ignore it as best we could and go about falling in love, having families, and (most importantly of all) buying products that were supposed to make our lives easier and happier? Although not the first to point it out, in her book *Acedia and Me: A Marriage, Monks, and a Writer's Life* American writer Kathleen Norris calls this time the "postwar triumph of both weapons-making and consumer manufacturing." Might the one have existed without the other?

In the timeline of my story we're edging up towards the nightmare that was the Cuban Missile Crisis, when more than a few of us felt the cold, truly frightening reality of the imminence of all-out nuclear conflagration. But I rather suspect that while it dealt a mighty blow to our complacency, it had only short-term consequences; its social and political reverberations eventually died down, and we settled back down into the pretence of trying to live as if the sword of nuclear annihilation wasn't hanging over our heads, and got busy being good consumers and buying things again. Those swords, though, have never been beaten into ploughshares. They hang there still.

What my father and so many others did as this all played out wasn't part of the flashier stories that Hollywood preferred; no one wanted to see a movie about someone sitting and staring at a radar scope looking for a telltale blip that would indicate either the imminence of Armageddon or a large flock of birds. What my father did – and by that I include why he left his family for periods of time, and where it was he would end up going to work – could be seen as being very loosely a part of the notion of sacrifice drummed into our heads. We think of those like my father who, earlier, had militarily participated in World War II as having sacrificed their youth and all too often their lives for, in our Canadian case, King and Country (that is, to ostensibly protect a way of life). Via an American propaganda machine that was and is Hollywood, we were consequently taught that it was necessary to do the same things for pretty much all the same patriotic reasons (now metonymically rephrased as Queen and Country) as World War II blurred into the Cold War – only this time not only were Western Values being threatened, but human existence as well.

And perhaps the biggest lie of all was the initial kernel of falseness that lay on the other side of a curtain we were never supposed to see behind, like in the *Wizard of Oz*. "Pay no attention to the man behind the curtain," I seem to recall the Wizard saying near the end of the film as Dorothy and her friends discover the truth about Oz. And many knew the truth about our nuclear Oz, about how those Soviet bombers I keep raising the spectre of never existed in anything remotely resembling the threatening quantity we were intended to believe by those who had a vested interest in having us believe thusly. It was called the bomber gap, and it was the apparent invention of intelligence agencies that vociferously and self-servingly argued the United States was being numerically outmatched by a vast fleet of Soviet bombers that, in fact, never existed. And when that ploy ultimately was demonstrated to be a lie, when someone decided to look behind the curtain and see what was there, it was recast by the same self-serving groups as a "missile gap": that now the Soviets had numerically superior quantities of intercontinental ballistic missiles that were to be aimed over the Pole, and were preparing to annihilate everything of Western Value. That, too, was a lie. At first. Eventually, those who argued such lies got their twisted little wishes granted as the Soviets were finally able to get up to speed production-wise and match the United States in

Armageddon potential. Both sides of this sorry little story consequently staggered forward into the weird, barely balanced world of what came to be known as "mutually assured destruction" – you attack me, I attack you, we all die – while the rest of us continued to be spoon-fed caricatures of Duty, Sacrifice, and the Greater Good.

So my father went to Great Whale River on the edge of Hudson Bay to work on the Mid-Canada Line, sacrificing his family life, and even something like other potential career paths he might have taken, for the greater good – yes? Well, no. Or maybe. Part of it is true, depending entirely on how one defines "greater good." My father arguably made sacrifices for the "greater good," though it certainly wasn't defined in his mind as something as hopelessly abstract as that of Queen and Country, or even the notion of Western Values, as it was the much closer and mundane reality of simply providing for his family. The short version of this is that he could earn better money in heading up to the fifty-fifth than he could have had he not gone north. He now had a wife and three children that constituted his immediate family, and being there for them in a hands-on, even emotional way wasn't a significant part of the bargain as the family unit was supposed to have been understood at the time. My father, again as with so many of his generation, was Dad, Breadwinner, not Dad, Emotional Supporter. The latter role was relegated entirely to mothers, to those who stayed behind and cleaned up the messes and did the exhausting, and often thankless, work of raising the children while Dad, Breadwinner, was elsewhere winning some better bread than was to be had had he just stayed home.

And so he went to where the Better Bread was, and in doing so dealt another blow – albeit an extremely minor one – to another propagandistic notion we carried about: that of the importance of the family. The notion of the nuclear family has come to be rendered synonymous with the threat of nuclear annihilation, and so both become integral parts of Cold War mythology: dad, mom, and two point whatever number of kids (and in that order of importance) who made up what was statistically imagined to be the typical nuclear family. It was all supposed to be about the Importance of Family, of Protecting the Family.

And yet the Cold War, by its very nature, routinely shredded the family to bits, no matter what nonsense movies or television showed us. My family was by no means unique in being torn apart so Dad could go – or could be unwillingly sent – to serve his country and protect the family somewhere where his family was not. Military life was that of routine disruption of the nuclear family, sacrificed to some other notion of serving the greater good. As a consequence, families routinely fell apart, marriages disintegrated, alcohol (which was so readily and cheaply made available on military bases) became a crutch that so many discovered far too very late was, of course, no such thing. How could such deterioration *not* happen? How could a family endure such an experience and stay whole? Many did. Mine, in the end, did not.

My father, Breadwinner, provided the finances that ensured that my mother, sisters, and I would always have a home, clothing, and food in our stomachs. We would want for nothing, for while he ensured that materially we were looked after, my mother would never fail us either, providing the emotional and psychological support and shaping of we children. But it was in the city of Windsor, and by extension at the military base of Great Whale River on the Mid-Canada Line (an entity which came to an end before my family did) where, I rather suspect, the seeds of familial destruction were sown as my mother must have come to the painful conclusion that she was essentially all on her own in raising her three (and, six years from now, four) children.

We've reached a narrative point where things begin to fall apart, where entropy begins to take its inevitable toll on what has been built. My family has been made, created (save for the last child), and from here on in things begin the incremental process of decay. The Mid-Canada Line is the tipping point for things familial, as the strains of living the military life begin to show.

Didn't take long.

Back at the sub-familial, individual level, though, my sisters and I still had much making to do. In Windsor, for instance, I had my first conscious encounter with gravity. It happens, ironically enough, in what was likely a building that my grandfather had been responsible for. During a shopping trip in downtown Windsor, my mother had taken me to a lunch counter in a department store – probably a Kresge's, and very likely one that my grandfather had designed when he worked for the company – and I had the rare privilege of having a soft drink. I drank my Coke from a paper straw, experiencing, I rather suspect, this simple technology for the first time in my life. Once I had been instructed on how to use this device to draw the drink up from the glass and into my mouth, I didn't know how to stop, afraid that once I'd started the liquid moving through the straw it would keep going on once I'd taken my mouth away from the end. I continued to drink more from fear than from pleasure, until my mother thought that I was being piggishly greedy and chided me. But I drank on, panicking, unable to break the connection, convinced that disaster would ensue and that the Coke would continue to pump up from the straw all on its own, spilling onto the table and all over my clothes. In annoyance my mother finally pulled the drink away from me, breaking the cycle of what I thought was perpetual motion within which I had become entrapped – breaking the spell.

In Windsor I felt gravity's pull. In Windsor I tasted physics. And in Windsor I began to sense identity.

Romper, bomper, stomper boo.
Tell me, tell me, tell me, do.
Magic Mirror, tell me today:
Have all my friends had fun at play?

The first television program I have any clear remembrance of is *Romper Room,* a children's show and a memory forever linked with Windsor. Watching it, I longed to hear Miss Flora (the show's teacher in the Windsor-produced version) say my name aloud and make me real as she peered through the magic mirror at us on the far side of the screen.

"I see," she would begin, and children's names would spill from her mouth.

Mine was never one. And though I was never seen, never felt the magic of my name spoken aloud on television, it's here on Ouellete Avenue straight up the road from the Detroit River that the hindsight of half a century tells me a self began to coalesce.

7

SAGE

6602 – 81st Street S.W., Tacoma, Washington. I lived here.

The picture was taken by my father as he stood across the street, beside our mailbox. The older two of my three sisters, Elizabeth and Danielle, are with him. I'm inside the house, looking out the dining-room window that's next to the garage. I'm sick and wearing a bathrobe. You can't see me. Just as well.

We first arrived in Tacoma in early 1963, the Easter before President John F. Kennedy was assassinated. My father was posted there as part of the small RCAF contingent at McChord Air Force Base. Having driven across the continent literally from one ocean to the other – for most of the trip on the American side of the border, and all of it in the late winter (en route we ended up snowed in at a roadside motel in Grand Forks, North Dakota, for a couple of days), we lived for a week or so in a Tacoma motel until my parents found the house of that moment, a place forever linked in my memory with my sister Elizabeth regaling Danielle and me with delightful lies of the vast bounty of Easter presents awaiting us at our new home. It and the house next door, where we eventually moved, were owned by the same man, a U.S. Air Force pilot who was a member of the 498th Fighter Interceptor Squadron (known as the "Geiger Tigers") and flew an F-106 Delta Dart interceptor jet, missile-equipped planes designed to fly at supersonic speeds so as to intercept and down United States–bound Soviet bombers long before they could arrive over their targets and drop their payloads – or so the theory went. He would periodically bring us gifts of king crab from trips he made up to Alaska. We lived in that first house for a little more than a year, and then moved next door into the green-and-white home of this black-and-white photograph where we stayed until our next transfer in 1967. That's the lawn I weeded by hand, the backyard in which I pitched my pup tent and sat on hot summer days thrilling to Charles Lindbergh's *The Spirit of St. Louis* borrowed from the bookmobile that periodically came through our neighbourhood. That's the porch on which my parents taught me not to be afraid of thunder and lightning. That's the driveway on which my friends and I set up old cardboard boxes to slalom around on our wooden skateboards. That's the garage in which I built my first kites and stumbled across my father's small, fascinating stash of *Playboy* magazines. That's the car that brought us to Tacoma from our Pinetree Line posting at RCAF Station Beaverbank in Nova Scotia. And that's the boat my parents bought while we lived in Tacoma and which we would end up towing back across a good chunk of the continent in the summer of 1967 to our next posting in North Bay, Ontario. But I'm getting ahead of myself.

McChord and Tacoma are where I locate my favourite memory of my father. We were here because of an air force base created in 1930 that played a role in the Alaskan and Pacific campaigns of World War II (some of the airmen involved in Doolittle's bombing raid on Japan trained here). McChord also played a role in the movement of troops and matériel to Korea in the early 1950s during that war. And in the period in which we were stationed there, it played a significant role in the ongoing airlift of U.S. troops and military matériel to what was then South Vietnam. The very midst of this place and difficult time is where this memory was built and resides – in the living room of our house, on a numbered street, in this city of the Pacific Northwest, in the mid-1960s during the escalation of a war in which more bombs would be dropped than during all of World War II, but which would inevitably be lost and badly scar the psyche of a nation as a result. Our home in the Lakewood area of Tacoma was in a tract housing development called Robin Hood Estates situated on the northwest side of McChord. My copy of the *Guide to McChord* for 1962 that my parents acquired upon our move there describes it in typically overwrought real estate-ese as "Tacoma's newest area for discriminating home buyers ... fashioned from one of the loveliest of the private estates in the popular Lakewood District." The development was at the edge of something resembling nature: a nearby stream in which salmon would run each year (and which my buddies and I would occasionally catch with our hands just because we could) and bordered on its far side by a game farm we spent a lot of time wandering around in, watching the salmon raised there being stripped of eggs and sperm, and a place to which I would often go alone to draw the caged birds kept there; alliterative fields full of pheasant, the feathers of which I would find in the tall grasses and stick ballpoint pen refills into and pretend they were old-fashioned quill pens; and a forest – lush, damp, and vibrantly green (a shade I vainly and foolishly sought in North Bay for many years following our transfer there) as is the wont in the Pacific Northwest, replete with Douglas firs, large ferns, and enormous banana slugs – bordered by fields in which some horses were kept that we would regularly feed with crab apples. My school – John Dower Elementary, a place which I entered towards the end of the Grade 1 school term and left at the end of Grade 5, reciting each morning the Pledge of Allegiance with my hand over my heart like every other kid without giving the problematic context any thought at all – was very close by, and in my neighbourhood were other Canadian military brats my age. But because of its proximity to the massive Fort Lewis Army Base (whose hospital I would get to know intimately well courtesy the usual childhood problems of illnesses and broken bones) on the western side of where we lived, and the equally massive McChord AFB on the eastern side, our neighbourhood was in large part composed of American military families, and this during the escalation of U.S. involvement in a war in Southeast Asia which infected absolutely everything about life there.

Case in point: Robbie Shults, one of my best friends in Tacoma, who lived on the same street several doors down from us. The highlight of my summer was when his cousin would come to stay with Robbie and his family, and we would – the three of us – ride around in the back of his parents' truck as his mom ran errands. Robbie lost his father in a plane crash in Khánh Hòa, South Vietnam, in April 1967 not long before we were transferred out (my parents kept copies of the program for his funeral service, and you can find his name – Roy Earl Shults, Jr. – on the Vietnam Veterans Memorial Wall in Washington, panel 18E, line 24, a casualty of one of the first crashes of what were then brand-new jet transport airplanes of the USAF, the C-141 StarLifter), and so of course absolutely everything changed.

And before that, there was the newlywed couple who lived a street over from us who took a shine to us neighbourhood kids. They fed us Sloppy Joes, and ended their lives together – and our meals and pillow fights with them – when he was shot down over North Vietnam and classified for years as MIA – Missing in Action – before his death was finally confirmed. I remember her first name: Penny. I don't remember his. But it will be somewhere on the Wall.

The make-believe games of war my friends and I played in those alliterative fields and forests of Lakewood – Cowboys and Indians, Allies and Nazis – coexisted with the coffins I saw being offloaded from a military airplane at McChord one evening, with Robbie's father's death, with Penny's husband's disappearance. But the bad stuff was mainly on television, safely distant and given a contextualizing sense of unreality by the banal advertisements and mindless television shows that framed the news. I saw coffins only once – a brief glimpse of tarmac, airplane and boxes in a gap between some buildings one evening when my parents took us for the huge treat of a meal out at the cafeteria on the air base. I remember this image in black and white, as if it exists on the edge of sliding over the precipice separating the things I really saw and felt from second-hand reports on news shows like Walter Cronkite and the *Huntley-Brinkley Report* of evening television. Maybe I'm afraid of remembering it in colour. I'm more afraid that somehow it's not true, that what I saw on television bled over and contaminated my memories of an important place and time in my young life, decolouring a little bit of them. Real or not, it clings to me.

Now, here, with a half-century of distance rushing past me, what's truly real, truly now, truly here, ever present, is the same anxiety that plagued me back then. Robbie's dad died. Penny's husband disappeared. And my guts knotted. This wasn't supposed to happen, was it? I breathed in and out, saw the news, watched local television clown J.P. Patches (whom I adored), ate my bowls of Cap'n Crunch, picked up my gun (plastic, with large red plastic bullets), put on my helmet (plastic, with a bit of fake fern camouflage tacked on), went out to the forest or to a trench we had dug, bit my nails, and watched the sky. Anxiety born on the Atlantic side of North

America gripped me hard on its Pacific, and never let go. Maybe it was something in the air.

Maybe you should ignore that last sentence, no matter the hint of truth in it. I seem to be trying hard to make metaphors out of this experience, and perhaps I can't be trusted. But the fact is Southeast Asia *was* in the air, here in Lakewood, Tacoma, just on the northeastern edge of McChord AFB in a lush, damp corner of America. I mean that literally and not metaphorically. My sky was military. Every day it was criss-crossed with low-flying Douglas C-124 Globemaster II transport planes, enormous two storey-high, propeller-driven beasts with funny black bulbous noses that housed radar units, and clamshell doors for loading cargo right beneath them that were the long-serving precursors to the kind of plane Robbie's father flew on and died in. Fondly intended or not, "Old Shakey" became their collective nickname, one assigned by those who flew them courtesy the intense and unrelenting vibrations induced by the four piston-powered propellers that kept them aloft. They'd be on their way to or from South Vietnam, carrying troops – mostly draftees, I suppose – and supplies one way, presumably homecoming soldiers and coffins the other. And they flew low over our neighbourhood, probably because we were right under the flight path into McChord, but I remember being told by someone that it was because the aircrews wanted their families in the area to know they were back, that they were okay – they'd made it home alive. How true is that? It makes for a good story, but I don't know for sure. What's real is the memory of standing in the street throwing around a toy balsawood glider, or goofing around in our backyard, or sitting in one of the trenches we'd dug readying for a Nazi assault, only to stop, to look up, and to begin shaking as my body and the ground beneath my feet began to harmonically sympathize with the fundamental frequency of four 28-cylinder, 3,800 horsepower, air-cooled engines roaring low overhead. Mine was the vestigial shudder, the last faint tremor of something awful happening somewhere far away. I bit my nails.

I bit my nails. Not the best of responses to stress, but hey, I was a fearful kid to start with, newly compounded and confused by the shift in the direction of things. What little I understood about how the world worked had been turned sideways. I had believed my life – my family's life – to be about the up and down of the world. The scary bits, the bits that brought us to Tacoma in the first place, the bits that accounted for our lives on the move and my father's job, had everything to do with the up and down that was north and south, with scary people who lived on the other side of the North Pole and who didn't like us for some reason. The Soviets would attack us from there – that was what ordered our lives along those horizontal lines of continental defence that were Pinetree, Mid-Canada, and DEW. My father was involved in a perpendicular war, and we lived with its consequences.

But in Tacoma I discovered something else, something that worked sideways. Vietnam wasn't part of the up of things I understood – it was off to the left, to the west, somewhere. But I didn't understand sideways; it wasn't a part of me – yet. In school I struggled with comprehending how maps worked. In one of my classes hung a standard Mercator projection map of North America – you know, the kind where the continent is depicted as seen from space. I saw the mighty maw of the Gulf of St. Lawrence opening to the Atlantic, and the river that then extended southwest from it – to the left and down – to join up to the Great Lakes in the continental interior, and from what I saw I understood that, logically, the waters of the Atlantic Ocean ran downhill, swallowed up by the mouth of the Gulf and down the throat of the St. Lawrence into the great stomach of the Lakes. And I pondered long and hard – verbalizing it only once in front of my classmates in an early incident of making a total fool of myself – about what happened to the salt of that ocean. Did enormous mounds of the stuff accumulate along the shores of the St. Lawrence River as it became the fresh water of the Lakes? Yeah, I had trouble with maps, with my image of how the world worked, with distinctions between up and down and sideways that had nothing at all to do with direction and everything to do with geopolitics. I struggled to understand, and, after learning shame and humiliation, learned to keep my mouth shut. I didn't know what questions to ask. No, that's not true. I didn't know *how* to ask them, so, for better or worse, silence was the option I chose. Just like dad?

Turn away to something better.

Here is the memory that matters to me, the gift that Tacoma gave me: my father standing in front of our living-room window painting a Christmas scene upon it. He did it each year we lived there, and in my mind I'm sitting on the chesterfield behind him and to his right watching him apply tempera paint to fill in the figures of the wise men he had already outlined in black upon the glass. Like my other memories of him, it has no soundtrack. I don't hear the noise of my sisters playing on the floor in a room we spent little time in; I don't hear my mother – maybe she is elsewhere in the house. Maybe the stereo is on, playing Christmas music from one of the records that the Firestone tire company would issue each year for the holiday (and which I still have), or one of Bill Cosby's records. But I don't hear Julie Andrews's voice, nor Fat Albert's. This is a silent scenario. There's a diffused grey light filtering through the window to frame my father, and he is to me more a darkened silhouette than a fully three-dimensional figure.

But it's here where I locate him, one of the rare places where I find some happiness simultaneous in both him and me. An innocence-versus-experience cliché can be built from this if you choose, for this memory is built upon a ground of all matters far less pleasant. The reason we were even here in this beautiful corner of the world in the first place had everything to do with what my father had been trained for, and where he had been assigned by his military taskmasters to spend his workdays: inside a piece of Brutalist architecture of the most extreme sort, a building designed not as some Modernist edifice of absolute truth to its materials (concrete), but one designed to be resistant to ("hardened," is the proper military terminology, if I remember correctly) a nuclear attack: an enormous, multi-storey windowless concrete cube known as a blockhouse located at McChord that was the SAGE building.

SAGE. It's an acronym for *S*emi-*A*utomatic *G*round *E*nvironment (or unofficially rechristened courtesy of the cynical humour of air-force personnel who dealt with it on a daily basis as "*S*oviets *A*lways *G*uaranteed *E*ntry," or "*S*omebody's *A*lways *G*etting *E*xcited") a funny and oddly uninformative name for what was essentially a complex military computer system that began its technological life in 1944 at the Massachusetts Institute of Technology as another early computer with the much-catchier name of "Whirlwind" originally commissioned as a flight simulator (a project known as the Aircraft Stability and Control Analyzer) by the U.S. Navy.

We're not talking about anything remotely like the desktops that started to become an integral part of our lives in the early 1980s, but rather a digital mainframe computer from days of yore, the largest ever built. The SAGE computers – each with the prosaic designation "AN/FSQ-7" – were monstrously gigantic machines that weighed in at well over 250 tons each, contained 55,000 vacuum tubes that did the electronic work of processing information (bushel baskets of spares were apparently kept close at hand to replace those tubes that burned out), and consumed a half-acre of floor space. They generated vast amounts of waste heat – so much so that heating the buildings that housed them was *never* an issue (though cooling them most certainly was). And each site where they were stationed – twenty-three of them, all but one located in the continental United States – had two such machines, just in case one failed. SAGE created a totally integrated electronic network for the defence of the continent, Before it, radar sites across the country – like that of our old home of Beaverbank – essentially operated all on their own, literally linked together only by telephone lines someone would use to send information by voice or teletype to a central site where decisions would be made about how to respond to what might have shown up on a distant radar operator's screen. This was the BC era – Before Computers – when what was termed "manual" radar plotting of targets and controlling of responses was the norm. And it wasn't a heck of a lot different than how it had been during World War II, when radar was new.

Needless to say, it didn't work very well anymore. In 1952, four years before I was born and when the Cold War was still a new and shiny toy, the shortcomings of these procedures became embarrassingly overt. Reports came in to McChord from Alaska indicating that some unknown aircraft had been spotted heading towards the lower forty-eight from the Bering Sea. The information was coupled with other reports about increased bomber activity in the Soviet Union, and was passed along through the military chain of command. When another report came in about unknown high-flying aircraft near Maine, all hell broke loose and the very first Air Defense Readiness Alert for the United States was ordered.

In the end, nothing came of it all – some of the aircraft were identified as commercial flights that were off-course – but the inordinate amount of time it took to sort everything out made it crystal clear that the system – such as it was – just didn't cut the proverbial mustard. Enter SAGE, a creation of MIT's Lincoln Labs, the postwar version of the university's legendary Rad Lab and the place where an awful lot of military technology was created.

Those are the facts, or some of them, anyway. But the "Semi-Automatic" nature of SAGE is important, for it meant that, despite the pivotal role of the massive military computers, human beings weren't entirely out of the information processing loop, and consequently people like my father – and there were a lot them – had a role to play in it all. Exactly *how* he fit into SAGE is something I've never been privy to. His service record lists him as being an "AD Tech" – Air Defense Technician – at the time. He was one of those people manning a system whereby a computer tracked things (often, flights of birds that were mistaken for something far less benign) via dedicated connections over telephone lines (using the very first modems) digitally sending and receiving incoming information from radar sites across the continent as the system and its operators went about their Cold War task of keeping an electronic eye out for incoming Soviet bombers carrying nuclear weapons attempting a first strike on North American targets.

Like a lot of other technology, SAGE was in large part outdated when it became operational (though it spun off a lot of other new technology, including the very first computer built with solid-state transistors instead of vacuum tubes, smaller by a long shot than its "hollow state" predecessor but by an equally long shot much larger than what became the desktop computer of the 1980s), for the Russian bombers it had been designed to keep tabs on had long

The McElroy family, Tacoma, Easter 1965

been superseded by a much more effective weapon: the intercontinental ballistic missile. And SAGE wasn't nearly as good at tracking those – they moved far too quickly, far too high, giving much less advance time to coordinate information and make decisions. Still, the system was up and running for a surprisingly long time; the SAGE facility in North Bay, Ontario, for instance – the only one not housed in a concrete cube but, rather, buried far underground, and the only one not located in the United States – was operational from 1963 until the early 1980s, when its AN/FSQ-7 computers (nicknamed "Bonnie and Clyde") were dismantled and pieces of them immediately transferred to a computer museum in California where they're exhibited as historically important examples of what had once been cutting-edge Cold War technology employed to defend North America.

This is what my father – and so many others – did during this part of the Cold War, and that's why our family – like so many others – spent some years of it in Tacoma. The Canadian contingent of folks like us stationed south of the border in this lovely little bit of America would hold a picnic every July 1 to celebrate what we knew back then as Dominion Day, gathering at – of all the ironically named places – American Lake, a pretty little spot adjacent to McChord and on whose shores was located a large veteran's hospital, where we would swim and eat and socialize. And our family would celebrate both Canadian and American Thanksgivings, something I loved as a child and which I do to this day still.

And in the four years we were in Tacoma, my father was around a lot. He had no temporary reposting while we were stationed there, and I have no remembrances of him as a drunken figure. He was more dad-like, and as a family we did a lot of things together. We made numerous trips – often accompanied by a couple whose backyard bordered on ours and with whom my parents had become quite close, people I can only remember as Bus and Jean – to the broad beaches of the Pacific where we would spend the day hunting razor clams. "Hunting" is the right term, as the clams were surprisingly quick creatures. So to catch one: reconnoitre the beach and look for a small dimple or crater in the wet sand, sign of a razor clam lurking just beneath the surface. Then quietly approach said crater and dig like mad. Experienced clammers had a shovel with a long narrow blade to maximize the depth of each shovel load. In the end it usually involved getting down on your hands and knees and plunging your arm down deep into the mysteries of wet sand and blindly feeling around for the clam which was trying like mad to get away. As a kid, that took some getting used to.

Such trips always involved a beach lunch of cold fried chicken and potato salad, and on our return my parents would clean the clams so that the next day my mom could make a huge batch of Manhattan clam chowder. (Despite having lived previously in Maritime Canada, it would be a while before I learned that there was another kind.)

On other trips, we would go to the Hood Canal (which isn't actually a canal at all, but rather a long narrow fjord that led out to what was called Admiralty Inlet, then to the Strait of Juan de Fuca, and finally out to the open Pacific) and watch U.S. Navy submarines go by heading either to port or to sea as we picked mussels or swam in a small tidal basin. Better yet, we'd go to Bremerton, just a short drive north that took us over the infamous Tacoma Narrows Bridge. I didn't know about its history – the bridge I mean – until a few years after we'd left the States and returned to Canada. In high school in North Bay my Grade 11 science teacher one day showed a grainy old black-and-white film of a suspension bridge twisting and turning in the wind, finally tearing itself to pieces and falling into the water far below. "Hey, I know where that is!" I said out loud, to the tittered amusement of some of my classmates. It was my bridge, but another, earlier incarnation that had come to be known as "Galloping Gertie."

My memories of the bridge always involve my fascination with the surging waters I could see far below as we drove across, and the fact that in Bremerton, on the far side of the bridge, was the Puget Sound Naval Shipyard. And ships. *Big* ships.

Bremerton was and is an important naval base on the West Coast. During our Tacoma posting, the USS *Missouri*, the enormous Iowa-Class battleship on which the Japanese officially signed the papers of surrender ending World War II, was mothballed out there (and I still remember my shock during the first Gulf War of the early 1990s when I learned that the *Missouri* had been reactivated and was serving on duty in the Persian Gulf); my friends and I ran around on its wooden deck, stood before the disk on the deck denoting the exact spot where the war had ended, and gazed in awe at the size of its anchors and mammoth guns. And my father once took the family on a tour of the aircraft carrier USS *Constellation*, her deck packed with cars and not airplanes, just before she set sail for southern California to pick up aircraft and weapons before heading out across the Pacific to Southeast Asia.

But Tacoma was more than all things military. A bunch of stuff was borderline: the aforementioned occasional meal at the base cafeteria (which was a huge treat, as it was one of the rare times we ate out and when I could have a hamburger); or the weekly trips to buy groceries at the McChord commissary, a place my sisters and I never saw the insides of as we were relegated to sitting in the car and waiting for our parents' return – that kind of thing. And despite living in a neighbourhood with a lot of military personnel, it was *not* like living on-base in a PMQ; the houses didn't all look the same, for starters. For the most part our lives were as close to being civilian as they could be: we had a view of the dormant volcano Mount Rainier and the chain of the Cascade Mountains framed through the sliding glass door of our family room; the friendships and meals with our neighbours, many of whom had absolutely nothing to do with the military; skating at a rickety old indoor ice rink that precariously cantilevered out over the steep shore of Gravelly Lake; exploring the woods around our home, and building forts or digging trenches with my friends (some military brats, some not); a trip to Portland, Oregon, to a boat show my father wanted to see but which had, for me, the added bonuses of seeing the Batmobile and eating a pizza afterwards; or fishing with my father and a friend on Lake Cushman, where I caught my very first trout ...

And it was in Tacoma that I learned of my father as someone other than that taciturn man I was afraid of; someone other than the distant and somewhat scary person living in our house who worked day or evening shifts and dressed in winter-blue or summer-green uniforms, who polished his shoes to a high sheen with old nylon stockings. I saw, instead, this man who stopped outside a neighbourhood supermarket to buy a pencil from a legless man sitting on the sidewalk, chatting with him for a few minutes and giving him a smile that rarely came my way. And I saw this guy who cared about stuff that had nothing to do with being my father. Like speedboat racing, and particularly those powerful hydroplanes that barely skim across the surface of the water at dangerously high speeds, occasionally catching too much air and spectacularly cartwheeling before being utterly destroyed upon impact with the water (and often killing their drivers in the process).

One summer he took me to Seattle – just me, no sisters – to watch the hydroplane competitions that were the main event of what was once a huge deal in the city, Seafair. He bought us passes – small plastic ship steering wheels that we pinned to our shirts – that gave us close-up access to the pit areas, and for a few days we sat on the grassy shore of Lake Washington under some shady trees watching boats like *Miss Bardahl* compete in time trials, and wandered through the pit areas looking close-up at the boats and the people involved with them. The day of the actual race itself we stayed home – the admission price too expensive, too much traffic, too many people – and, sitting side by side on the chesterfield in the family room, ate our supper off of TV trays as we watched the race broadcast live on local television. I've no idea who won, and hydroplane racing – or any racing, for that matter – never stuck as a lifelong passion with me.

Though I had an inkling at that time, the fact that this was a lifelong passion of my father's was something I would only learn of after his death thirty-some years after we sat on the shores of Lake Washington, when The Box was passed along to me. Here was something else I had only had the merest glimmer of until that time: the fact that my father was an amateur photographer, and had been since he was a teenager. As I sorted through the black-and-white prints and colour slides – all but a handful of them unlabelled, unidentified, unorganized (save for a mouldering old photo album into which a number of pictures that looked like they'd been taken in the Arctic had been glued, and carousels in which the slides were set) – images of speedboat racing fell into a natural grouping, pictures he'd taken of competitions on the Detroit River. Accompanying them was a scrapbook of press clippings he'd carefully saved from local newspapers, some just the tiniest little pieces of newsprint detailing what boats had participated in what heats. Here was my father's passion.

And as the pictures organized themselves and coalesced into something meaningful for me, our childhoods somehow intersected – just a little shard, for of his I know absolutely nothing beyond the only childhood memory he ever passed along to me: shovelling coal in the basement of his parents' house to fill a bin that fed the furnace (a home that I don't think my grandfather had designed and built). Like any child, I had wanted to please my father, to make his love entirely mine, even if my understanding of how to do that was limited by the mindset of a child. And so in Tacoma I had hung on to *Miss Bardahl* and her ilk and tried to make them important to me because even with my limited frame of reference I could see how important they were to him. And later – so much later as to really be in one sense far too late – because of some boats we had watched together in the mid-1960s from the edge of an urban lake in the Pacific Northwest, and because of some photographs he had taken years before I arrived on the scene thirteen days after he and my mother were married, his life – that shard of it, anyway – became superimposed upon mine. For a moment, I knew my father.

But I have no pictures of this. And the plastic ships' wheels are long gone.

8

DISTANT EARLY WARNING

The summer before he left my father and I fished.

Every evening after the supper dishes had been cleared away, we packed the car and drove up the escarpment that overlooks North Bay, behind the air force base, and then descended a dusty dirt road that led to a pump house on the shore of Four Mile Lake. A short walk led us to a large boulder at the water's edge, and from there we fished.

The thing about fishing is how little speech matters. The taciturn was a way of life for my father, and while I've no idea why, for much of it I was actually quite grateful; his silence spared me the possibility of an intimate, squirm-inducing conversation with a man I barely knew. On the rocky shoreline of Four Mile Lake, we cast our worm-baited hooks, tightened the lines, and then waited in the absence of words for the strike, the nibble, the dowsing of the rod tip as perch – our usual prey – found our bait, which my father immortalized in a photograph showing me holding a stringer full of perch in one hand, and the large two-pounder I'd caught that day in the other. In our word-emptied silence, I would stare, mesmerized, at my rod, at its tip as the wind-rippled surface of the lake flowed along just out of focus behind it.

No, that's not quite right. "Absence of words" isn't true, nor is "word-emptied." They imply that something had been and was now gone, and that wasn't the case at all. Our mutual discomfort with one another – me, a lonely thirteen-year-old; him, a perhaps equally lonely forty-seven-year-old man – meant that we didn't lapse into silence at the lake. Silence was, instead, the very basis of our relationship. It was our bedrock. So in our realm of non-speech, we fished every evening of the summer and each weekend through the early fall of 1969, bringing home our catch to gut and then give the fillets to my mother, who froze them in meal-sized containers.

I don't recall if I knew then that my father was soon to leave. Maybe I've chosen not to remember. Just the merest flicker of memory ripples through my mind of a difficult, conversation in my bedroom, a memory of intense discomfort as, me sitting at the edge of my bed, my father sat on my desk chair and said something to me about growing up. Was this just before he left? Probably – the bedroom of that memory fits the time period, so I will say, yes, this is me remembering my father telling me he was to leave.

And the fact is that on the surface I was probably relieved to know he would become an absence. Military life had long meant that he worked shifts and, I recall, when even younger, being most comfortable when he worked evenings and I wouldn't have to sit sobbing in front of him being drilled on the multiplication tables as he grew ever more frustrated, ever more angry. But this absence was different, and I know I didn't understand then just how it would be so, for the view from hindsight quite clearly tells me: this was the last time my father would live with us as a family.

I don't, however, remember my father actually leaving. But in November 1969, in the midst of the misery that was the eighth grade, he did just that, heading for Winnipeg and from there, to the Arctic, where he was to become a "DEW Liner." So the photograph, here, is of him at a place known as Hall Beach on the edge of the Melville Peninsula in what was then the Northwest Territories but what is now Nunavut, at a DEW Line station called FOX Main. It's September 1970. He's about to turn forty-eight – old for a DEW Liner, who generally tended to be much younger men and women as evidenced in some of the photographs he takes up north – and is starting his second year on the Line, though in November his military tour will finish and he will retire from the Canadian Forces (which the RCAF, the Royal Canadian Navy, and the Canadian Army had become with unification of all three branches in 1968) prior to what would likely have been a transfer to the Pinetree Line base at Senneterre, Quebec, near Val d'Or. And, like a lot of ex–air force types, he will stay on the Line and go to work for the civilian contractor responsible for the whole kit and kaboodle, FELEC Services, an offshoot of Federal Electric, the service arm of the mighty corporation International Telephone & Telegraph (ITT). He gets his foot in the door as a switchboard operator being paid $3.40 an hour, but will quickly work his way up to becoming integral to the Line's logistics operations. This happens when I'm fourteen and am enduring my own transition: I've started high school.

It's been a little more than three years since we'd returned to Canada in July 1967, Centennial Year, transferred from Tacoma, Washington, on the U.S. West Coast to North Bay, in northeastern Ontario – another SAGE–based posting for my father. Again we drove, travelling across the country – this time, via the Canadian route and in the summer – with me and two of my sisters sitting in the back seat, and, in front, my mom, dad, and baby sister, Renee, who'd been born the year before. Behind the car, we hauled our boat loaded down with supplies we would need for the trip.

In those days, SAGE mattered a great deal, and as a result families like ours were shuttled around the country to ensure that the system was kept operational; actual human beings were still deemed consequential in keeping the information flowing for this computerized system of air defence. Of all the SAGE centres, North Bay was the only one situated outside the United States, coordinating information accumulated by Pinetree Line radar sites (like Beaverbank and St. Margaret's) as well as by the DEW Line, so as to monitor the airspace in the vast Canadian north keeping watch out for you-know-who. And it had one further distinction: instead of being housed in a nuclear-hardened, above-ground concrete structure like the one at McChord AFB, at Canadian Forces Base North Bay, SAGE computers and the people who kept them running were buried underground in the rock of the pre-Cambrian Shield. So rather than working in a windowless concrete bunker, my father worked in an *underground* windowless concrete bunker.

The base at North Bay has its origins in World War II, when it became part of the network of sites used to ferry aircraft from North America to Europe. A postwar RCAF station was formed here in 1951, and it became home to squadrons of jet interceptor aircraft. In the late 1950s, it was decided to locate a SAGE site here. Colloquially known as "The Hole," it dates back to August 1959, when crews began its construction working twenty-four-hour days and six-day weeks, blasting their way six hundred feet down through the ancient rock of the escarpment atop which the military base sat. It endured a week-long strike by electricians in the summer of 1962, and finally became a working military site in October 1963. It was a vast underground structure comprised of five separate caverns, two mile-long roadways to the surface along which buses transporting people operated, and a five-million-gallon water reservoir for cooling the two vacuum tube–powered computers. Not too far away, atop the same escarpment into which The Hole had been carved, a squadron of nuclear-tipped, surface-to-air Bomarc missiles were established in 1961 as a defence mechanism to intercept and bring down incoming Soviet bombers; its nuclear arsenal arrived from the United States two years later, airlifted in via those same bulbous-nosed, clamshell-doored C-124 Globemaster cargo planes that filled my Tacoma skies. (The transfer by ground of one shipment of warheads from the air force base to the Bomarc site entailed driving down the escarpment into the city and then back up along another road, as no direct road connected the two. The timing of the ground transfer coincided with a small earthquake in the city, leading many panicked people to believe that a nuclear accident had occurred.) The Bomarcs comprised only one of two such squadrons in Canada (the other was in La Macaza, Quebec) that were both finally shut down in 1972. All of the North Bay site – the nuclear-hardened Hole, the presence of nuclear-equipped missiles, an air base that could handle large aircraft easily – would mean that I would end up taking some bleak, teenage comfort in the knowledge that should a war break out, here in North Bay we lived at the centre of a geopolitical bull's eye that ensured we would be utterly annihilated; consequently, I wouldn't have to worry about surviving the initial devastation of such an unimaginable conflagration. I know I wasn't alone in thinking this way.

Welcome to the Cold War.

Our move to this place of the potential of strangely comforting nuclear devastation from another place of much the same potential – to North Bay from Tacoma – was preceded by a postcard and copy of the local newspaper mailed to us by friends who had been posted there a few months before our move. I remember noting with horror that the newspaper had only a quarter-page of comics, wondering what fresh hell we were being sent to (or less literary thoughts to that effect). My mother set to work drilling me on the names of the provinces and relearning the words to "God Save the Queen," which I hadn't sung since the first grade at our Pinetree Line posting of Beaverbank. It all meant nothing to me, for I was, but for the facts of my birth and citizenship, dual French and Canadian at the time, an American (I still remember the words to the Pledge of Allegiance). Little of Canada had stuck to me through our four years in the United States; it hadn't settled into my bones before we left the country in 1963. But readying to come back to Canada in 1967, I had to relearn my foreignness.

We departed Tacoma after the school year had finished. The day we left was emotional. In the early morning, we said our tearful goodbyes to my parents' best friends, Bus and Jean, and then hit the road to the British Columbia border and back into Canada. The plan had been to make for Kamloops the first night. We never made it, staying instead at a cottage somewhere on what I think must have been the Coldwater River, me and Elizabeth and Danielle sharing a bed sleeping the wrong way across it. I was heartsick. Many of my friends from Tacoma had already been transferred out, so it wasn't missing them that made the tears flow. It was the loss of some certainty in my life. We – my sisters, my mother, even my father – had been cut adrift. Again. We were heading back out into the unknown.

Again.

The drive took us ten days through the early summer of 1967. Each morning, we were up for sunrise and drove for an hour or so as the day lightened. We'd stop for a short break for breakfast somewhere on the road after which we would drive until mid-afternoon, when we would stop for the day so everyone could relax a bit. The prairies were blisteringly hot. My baby sister's poopy diapers stank up the car. After a flat tire briefly halted us in the then-bleak and utterly denuded moonscape of Sudbury, we paused only briefly in North Bay, where my father reported to the base and where we unhitched the boat we'd towed across country. We then drove south to Windsor and my grandparents' home on Riverside Drive, where my mother, sisters, and I would spend the remainder of the summer while my father returned to North Bay to work and to ostensibly look for a place for his family to live. My grandparents were, needless to say, less than thrilled to have their son's wife and children dropped into their laps.

Again.

The summer of 1967 was the third time my father had left us in Windsor, the second time he had left us at his parents' home. I wasn't a stupid kid; even I could see that we weren't welcome. Three boisterous children, a baby, and that foreign woman who had married their son were not my grandparents' idea of house guests. (I still have a vivid memory of my grandfather forcing me to pick up my baby sister's poop from the dining-room floor with bare hands.) Knowing no one, I spent my days alone sitting on the front step, watching the river traffic across the road. Back then, the St. Lawrence Seaway was a busy shipping lane, so ships were always passing up or down the Detroit River – mostly ore or grain carriers, but once I saw an American submarine – that I would try to identify by the flags on their sterns or the company logos on their smokestacks. In the evenings, the parade of shipping traffic would be joined by the colourfully lit Bob-Lo Boats cruising upriver from Detroit to a popular amusement park on Bois Blanc Island at the mouth of Lake St. Clair and back again.

That year, 1967, was also the summer of the riots in Detroit, and my grandparents' riverfront home offered me a front-porch view of America on the verge of tearing itself apart. Over the course of five violent days that July, days during which dozens of mostly young

African-American men were shot or beaten to death and hundreds more hurt, I watched black smoke rise from downtown across the river and chewed my fingernails. At night, I could hear sirens and see the flashes of police-car lights. I'm sure of those sounds and sights, but less sure of the memory of the sound of gunfire which also clings to me. Did I actually hear that? Could I have? Can I trust this memory? I'm not at all sure; maybe it all depends on the kinds of questions I ask of it (like: do I *want* to remember it this way?). I am certain, though, of the shape of my fear, tangible as it was in my gut. We'd left one place that peripherally echoed of a war zone; now it appeared we were in another – and this time even closer. This wasn't the cold comfort I would later take in obliterating nuclear conflagration that I would likely have very little warning of. This was about the knowing immediacy of pain and terror – of impending chaos. Here, in Windsor of all places, I could watch smoke rise, watch people come and gather at spots along the river looking at what little they could see across the river, and thought – imagined? – I could hear gunfire. I bit my nails, my body rippling with anxiety, and at night I would stand by my bedroom window in the dark desperately trying to bear witness to – even partake of from a distance – something resembling normalcy: I would watch a neighbour in the house next door sit at his kitchen table reading his newspaper until the anxiety eased enough that I was able to finally sleep.

We lasted about a month or so in Windsor before my mother put her foot down and insisted my father – who was apparently enjoying his bachelor existence in North Bay, drinking heavily again – come and rescue us. We left in early August. As we still had no home, we spent the month before school started living at a rundown establishment called the Bluebird Cottages on Lake

Nipissing. It was one of the last remnants of the old tourism in the area that had been kick-started some thirty years earlier by the roadside attraction of the Dionne Quintuplets born not far away. Our ramshackle cottage on the edge of the lake had two bedrooms in which my parents and two of my sisters slept. I had the couch in the living room next to my baby sister's crib. After the dismal month at my grandparents' home, it was liberating, despite the nightly crying of my baby sister a couple of feet away. My sisters and I spent a glorious month playing on the beach and splashing in the warm, shallow water of the lake. Sometimes in the cool of the evening we would drive by the enormous trailer of our moving company parked on a downtown North Bay street that contained all our worldly belongings, locked up and sealed by Customs, as we waited for a home.

On the first day of school, we moved into a rented home in the north part of town far from the lake, and that year – in September 1967 – I went back to school and restarted my Canadian education, interrupted by four American years, the day after everyone else. Besides being the new kid, my differences were pointedly highlighted at once by the French teacher, who recognized everyone else in her class except me, and who asked me to stand up and respond to her French questions. Having spent the last four years being taught Spanish, I stood mute, uncomprehending, and humiliated. Eventually, she had me count to ten *en français*, repeating each of the unfamiliar words after her, to the great amusement of my classmates. It was not an auspicious beginning. That morning I was closely inspected and found wanting, and I soon earned a nickname – "Moose" – that had everything to do with the fact that I was fat.

We spent eight months in that home – months during which

I learned to skate again (badly), and played my first, shaky games of hockey. That Christmas, my father presented me with a jockstrap and cup that, when he asked if I knew where it went, I put up against my face like a mask, out of sheer embarrassment at having to admit to either him or my mother *any* knowledge of my private anatomical bits. I also got my first and only pet dog. And then we moved again, back down to the south end of the city, to an old house my parents bought, the first our family ever owned. And so my two school-age sisters and I spent the last two months of the academic year at a new school. I was the new kid again, but at least my nickname had been left behind.

This was the house – 107 Lakeshore Drive – where I would reach puberty, develop dysentery, experience the Hong Kong flu, watch my first solar eclipse (partial) through a piece of cardboard pierced with a pin, see my mother go out early one morning and teach a bunch of municipal employees clearing ditches how to properly use a scythe, and learn what it was to be bullied. This was the house in which we lived when my father and I fished, and from where he left in November 1969 for the DEW Line.

~

The Cold War beckoned again, but it was the disintegration of my parents' marriage – sealed with a formal separation agreement I saw years after it had been drawn up – and the prospect of making good money to support his family (for my father did many things, but he never abandoned us financially) that took him north – not any great belief in the sacrifices needed to defend Western democracy from the evils of Communism. (Indeed, towards the end of his time on the Line nearly twenty years later, it amused him that the electronic equipment at DEW Line sites – much of it, apparently, old vacuum-tube technology that had long been rendered archaic by solid-state circuitry – was kept in working order by purchases of replacement tubes from one of the few places where they were still manufactured: the Soviet Union.)

The DEW – short for Distant Early Warning – Line, but originally known as Project 572 during its construction phase, was my father's Cold War military hat trick: a posting to the third and final line of defence set up against any possible Soviet attack across the North polar region. It's gone now, replaced by the North Warning System which does pretty much the same thing but requires far fewer people to run. But along with the nuclear bomb it epitomized the Cold War. After my father's death, as I began to belatedly try and understand something about who he was and what he'd been a part of, I became a little bit of a DEW Line connoisseur, collecting any material I could find about this project that figured so largely in both his life and mine. Surprisingly little has been written – a few books of no great depth, some analytical academic material, magazine articles, that sort of thing. The prize possession of my small collection would have to be a seventy-one-page typewritten press manual prepared jointly by the RCAF, USAF, and the Western Electric Company, who built the Line, for a press tour organized for March 26 to April 3, 1956 (a little more than a year before construction was completed), detailing what could and could not be reported on ("The specific function of any unit or section of the chain is objectionable for release," it reads on the very first page of the manual). I found it tucked away in the back of a filing cabinet at the Highway Book Shop outside Cobalt, Ontario.

But most of my collection comprises articles from different sources, like "DEW Line: Sentry of the Far North," a photo-illustrated article that appeared in the July 1958 issue of *National Geographic* that tells some of the stories of the construction of this behemoth, rather romantically overwrought at times (phrases like "setting foot on terrain that had never felt even the mukluk of an Eskimo became an everyday occurrence"). A supervisor on the construction phase of the Line, for instance, is quoted about the difficulties experienced with the harsh environment, telling of landing in a small airplane "against a wind that almost matched our air speed. The plane rolled less than six feet after it touched the ground."

That the building of the DEW Line was a brutal campaign is unquestioned. It ranks as one of the biggest construction projects ever undertaken with massive sea- and airlifts of men and materiél that included 20,000 construction workers, 460,000 tons of material, 77,000,000 gallons of fuel, 22,000 tons of food, and even 100,000 copies of operational and maintenance manuals. And it all started at exactly the same place where SAGE was born: Lincoln Labs, a post–World War II offshoot of the Massachusetts Institute of Technology. (Funny how so much of my father's life ended up being shaped by an American university; first MIT's wartime Rad Lab, and then its Lincoln Labs. I really should get around to sending them a thank-you card.) In 1952, some serious minds set to thinking about how to best defend against the Soviet threat. Jimmy Doolittle's point made at the end of World War II about the then-new peril posed on the far side of the Arctic had become accepted military and political doctrine; the early-warning and interceptor guidance system that was the Pinetree Line roughly paralleling the U.S.–Canada border, along the forty-ninth parallel, was in the initial stages of construction, and the Mid-Canada Line that would eventually be constructed along the fifty-fifth parallel wouldn't be on the table for a while yet. But it was acknowledged that detection of Soviet nuclear-equipped bombers at such comparatively southern locations would be too late to stop them. Something farther north was needed.

U.S. President Harry Truman agreed, and just before the end of his presidency gave approval to the project. Soviet testing of its first nuclear weapon in August 1953 lent the project a sense of urgency and, in late 1954, Western Electric was given three years and bucketloads of American money to build the Line (for though most of the Line was on Canadian soil, the American military paid the full tab for its construction).

The DEW Line was set up roughly across the seventieth parallel from Alaska all the way to Baffin Island in the Canadian Arctic. The idea behind it was simple: a chain of radar stations would keep an electronic eye out for Soviet bombers and provide a few precious minutes' advance warning should bombers sweep across the Pole on their way to wreak havoc on the American industrial heartland. (Two chains of defence had originally been envisaged before plans were scaled back to the one.) Construction work began in 1955 (and once gravel airstrips had been established, a lot of supplies were flown into sites by those workhorse Globemaster cargo planes on which the USAF of the time depended heavily, and which consequently keep popping up in this story), and Western Electric met its deadline, handing over the proverbial keys on July 31, 1957. Six main stations comprised the Line (four of which were in Canada), with intermediate and auxiliary sites spaced in between. Every eighty kilometres had a Doppler radar installation – like the ones that comprised the Mid-Canada Line – forming a kind of electronic fence that would detect anything crossing through its beams. Main and auxiliary stations had rotating radars housed in geodesic domes, and enormous, multi-storey curved reflectors. Their giant bowed-in walls served as antennae for the tropospheric scatter-microwave

Globemaster cargo plane of Georgia Air Guard at Hall Beach DEW *Line site*

communications system used before satellites became ubiquitous presences in our skies to send information southward, bouncing signals off irregularities in the lowest layer of our planet's atmosphere.

And the same old problem reared its head: the bombers for which the DEW Line had been built never materialized – indeed, never existed. Instead, the incessant drive of wartime technology led (he said again) to even further technological development, this time to the intercontinental ballistic missile and reduced warning times of an incoming attack from many minutes to many, many fewer.

~

Still, a huge investment had been made in defence technology, and the DEW Line soldiered on, each station a kind of small world of its own. The image we tend to retain of this early idea of an electronic fence, what lingers in popular culture as symbolizing or epitomizing this historical entity, is that of Arctic darkness and howling winds beating against the shape of a geodesic dome holding fast against the elements.

Well, that's almost right. Buckminster Fuller's geodesic domes were (and, in fact, still are) used to shelter sensitive electronic equipment like radar from the elements. And their presence on the DEW Line was indeed ubiquitous. Originally, though, Western Electric used inflatable rubber domes to shelter sensitive radar equipment. But if the air blowers used to keep the dome inflated failed, the rubber material could collapse on a rotating piece of sophisticated technology. It would be the dome that would take the brunt of the damage, being torn apart as the radar turned beneath it. Not something you wanted to occur at an isolated spot, especially in difficult weather (it happened, for instance, at a mountaintop Pinetree

Typical DEW Line site with view of geodesic dome

Line station). So here's where Fuller's clever geodesic dome comes into its own.

It's 1972 and I'm sixteen years old. I have on near-permanent loan from my high-school library *The Whole Earth Catalog*, a compendium of information on living alternatively in the world. I desperately want to be a hippie. Part of it stems back to an incident in the summer of 1967, when we lived with my grandparents in Windsor. Every summer of our time in Tacoma my father would take me down to a barbershop when school let out for the summer break and have my head shaved. I spent those summers in hateful crew cuts my father forced on me during our summers in Tacoma. When we moved and my father left us in Windsor with my grandparents, I saw my chance. I asked my mother if I could let my hair grow out. She agreed, and I went to a barbershop by myself for a trim, where the barber didn't listen to my instructions but instead sheared my head. I left the shop in tears, and outside, sitting on a wall, encountered my first hippies. I remember only one of them vividly: a young man with long, shoulder-length blond hair and round metal-framed granny glasses. I vowed that would be me someday. It was. Cut back to 1972 and my dalliance with *The Whole Earth Catalog*. By then I was determined to be a writer, and I was going to be a writer who lived an alternative lifestyle as a hippie in what all hippies lived in: a geodesic dome, of course.

By the mid-1960s, the dome had become, for a lot of us, synonymous with the back-to-the-land movement. We'd forgotten – or more likely never knew – that the dome had a previous life as a piece of military technology. Oh, Buckminster Fuller didn't devise the dome for the military per se, but he quite successfully marketed it to them. The geodesic dome entered the world of the military via the Marine Corps, who first showed interest in its military application,

Tropospheric communications antennae at Cape Dyer

and moved along the chain to the Strategic Air Command of the U.S. Air Force. Not long afterward, the American State Department took a great interest in it as well, and domes ended up being used as American pavilions at international trade fairs, like the one held in Kabul, Afghanistan, in 1956, where the dome erected there (a last-minute replacement for the temporary tents usually employed) became wildly popular with visitors. The U.S. government saw that Fuller's dome could be used as propaganda – could be contextualized so as to be rendered synonymous with the idea of American freedoms and ingenuity – and so domes began to sprout up everywhere. The most famous was probably the American pavilion at Expo 67 in Montreal, a dome which still stands. I would argue – and I'm in no way the first – that Buckminster Fuller's clever engineering of geometry is itself a pretty potent symbol of all that was the Cold War.

So in 1972, at the age of sixteen, I sit on my bed with the library copy of *The Whole Earth Catalog* resting in my lap dreaming of dome days. I would sit in my own dome, and there be a writer. And while I did this, my father was several thousand miles farther north in the Arctic, there essentially because a geodesic dome made the ideal shelter for the radar that was keeping an eye out for anything Soviet and incoming across the polar ice cap. It was an irony I wouldn't appreciate – or even notice – for another thirty-seven years.

~

In the end, my father would spend years spanning three decades on the DEW Line at places like Hall Beach (FOX Main), where the picture of him was taken (the station's geodesic dome is in the far background just to the left of his head, and next to it are two huge

Hall Beach DEW Line station during Sealift with ships arriving to offload supplies and aircraft flying in

tropospheric scatter-communications reflectors for bouncing radio waves off of); Cape Dyer (DYE Main) on Baffin Island; Cape Parry (PIN Main) in the Northwest Territories, a location also used by NASA as a rocket-launch facility; and Cambridge Bay (CAM Main) in Nunavut. Places with code names were his home for all that time, and he was forced south back to his family in the late 1980s only by the Line's impending closure and the transformation of the remnants into the North Warning System, and by age.

By his own account, he spent the last few years of the DEW Line's existence moving from site to site – even more dispossessed than he had been before – presumably helping get things in order, because that was his civilian job: he worked logistics. I've a handful of pictures (some slides, some photographic prints) of him at this work, sitting behind his desk surrounded by shelves full of large binders, in some sporting a bushy white beard that exists solely in images, for I knew him only as a clean-shaven military man.

Of the handful of his DEW Line patches – you know, those stitched badges worn on, say, a jacket, that acknowledge everything from participation in high-school athletics, to achievements in the Scouting movement, to involvement in NASA shuttle missions – one is specific to his civilian job working logistics. It's made of felt and shaped like the head of a fox to acknowledge a DEW Line sector (a group of places known as FOX Sites), and is emblazoned with the words "FOX LOG[istic]S THE DEW LINE'S AWFUL POWER," and the image of a man's hand giving the finger.

Of all his patches – even the military ones that date back to World War II and his Chain Home postings – this is the only one that has loose threads attached. It was obviously once sewn on a jacket, but I never saw my father *ever* sport a patch on his clothing (or give anyone the "fuck you" sign, for that matter). I think it's

Landing craft used for Sealift operation,

Hall Beach

a reasonable guess that he acquired this one second-hand from someone else who did what he did.

So I picture him at his job talking on the telephone, typing at the teletype machine, ensuring that the station (or maybe, stations) had what they needed. On his yearly trips south and home, he would sometimes try to lure me north for the summer to earn the good money working "Sealift," the yearly major resupply of stations done by ships in the brief ice-free opportunity offered by the late arctic summer (back in 1956 during construction of the Line, a flotilla of seventy-eight ships had taken part). I never took the bait, and I wonder now why he repeatedly asked: did he just want to spend time with his son? I feared the criticisms of a man who only once in my life told me he was proud of me, just as I was about to start university, and for whom I could never seem to manage to do anything right. Did he realize all of this? Did he regret? Was he trying to reach out as best he knew how? And did he realize at some point that it was far too late, that he had lost me forever? I haven't a clue.

Every year, he came south from the Line for several weeks of vacation. Our lives as individuals and as a family had moved on without him in the meantime. Everything – *everything* – had changed. Right after he left, in the winter of 1969–70, my mother hired a woman to teach her to drive; I can still vividly remember sitting at the kitchen table on a frosty winter morning eating breakfast with my sisters and hearing my mother and her instructor backing our car – standard transmission, mind – out of the garage. This was the moment of her liberation from the old order. She would go on to work outside the home (she had a very busy business as a seamstress previously), and there would be new men in her life who would of course figure into the lives of my sisters and me – three, actually, two of whom I hated, the last of whom I liked and even loved. As

I edged closer to high school, Bobby Kennedy and Martin Luther King had been assassinated, the *Apollo* astronauts had made it to the moon (and I remember standing in the wintery schoolyard awaiting, with a group of other desperate kids, rescued by the school librarian Ruth Thib – yes, she needs to be named – who would make the school library a refuge from the bullies on the playground, staring into the intensely blue sky at the pale moon marvelling that astronauts had actually circled it, let alone later landed on it). This was my introduction to the fact that the world was both amazing and horrific, all at the very same time. I finally understood – sort of. Alas, such knowledge did nothing to stop the punches, the black eyes, the tripping, the stolen lunches and money. The compassionate intervention of a school librarian, of Ruth Thib, did far more.

I entered high school in the fall of 1970 registered incorrectly. Someone had screwed up my name, and as some horribly misshapen version of it was spoken into a microphone before the entire student body on my first day to the great amusement of all, I refused to respond. I stood in the auditorium as everyone filed out to their classes, rooted in place by equal doses of fear and humiliation, unwilling to acknowledge the appalling error as being about me, finally rounded up by a teacher and taken to the office where the misshapen name was reassembled into mine. I was then escorted to my class, where every eye turned upon me as the teacher pronounced aloud my non-name to, again, the amusement of all before giving me back my identity.

I had no big picture to wrest some comfort from, to know that in fact this moment would be my adolescent nadir and that life would slowly, incrementally get better. Of course I didn't know this then. I had no father to whom I could have spoken my anguish and fear even had I wanted to do such a personally unlikely thing, and my budding teenage discomfort would never have allowed me to speak of these things with my mother, though she had always been our family's emotional support. I was at my fourth school in the span of the three years we'd been back in Canada, and as teenage hormones began to reassemble me, my anger about it all grew exponentially. In a year, we would move yet again to our third home in four years and something resembling stability would finally begin to be forged. It would be the home where I would dream of dome days and where, in the stillness of a period of non-transience I'd never before known, a toxic combination of teenage angst and resentment towards my father would stew and simmer, and eventually become a destructively palpable presence in my life.

9

PARKA

My father may have been a watcher, but I'm a listener. Radio was a fundamental part of my life growing up, and as a teenager I became fascinated with what I could hear of world events on the shortwave frequencies. Listening to broadcasters like Radio Moscow, BBC World Service, and the Voice of America was a regular part of my life throughout the Cold War.

It's end, consequently, was an aural experience for me as I listened to, say, Radio Deutsche Welle broadcasting from what was then West Germany give the blow-by-blow of the crumbling of the Iron Curtain separating Western Europe from its Soviet-dominated neighbours, and the more literal destruction of the Berlin Wall itself. As the end of the Cold War became inevitable, the hopeful optimist in me actually thought that the world would become a safer place, and that my fear and anxiety would at last ease. My cynical side knew better, and framed how I listened to the June 1989 massacre of peacefully protesting students at Tiananmen Square in Beijing by a brutally repressive regime that would tolerate no dissent, and in January of 1991 heard the chillingly calm words of a Kol Israel radio announcer telling "local listeners" to immediately move to the sealed rooms in their homes as Iraqi missiles (which, it was initially feared, might have carried biological or chemical weapons) began to fall on Israel as the Gulf War began.

So much for the end of anxiety. The end of the Cold War

served only to unleash the dragons of pent-up regional and ethnic tensions. Yugoslavia tore itself apart as the world stood by and did virtually nothing except ensure that the words "ethnic cleansing" entered our everyday vocabulary, and that I would watch the evening news and weep at the sight of emaciated Bosnian prisoners and mass graves until my news addiction grew unbearable and the knot in my gut achieved permanence.

Over here in fortress North America, some Cold War symbols managed to disappear. By the end of the 1980s, the last of its great lines of electronic defence had become a part of history. Save for the remnants of a few bases still around serving other purposes, most Pinetree Line sites were inactivated from the mid-1970s to the early 1990s (a few, like Beaverbank, even as early as the 1960s) as they were rendered superfluous and archaic courtesy technology's relentless march forward. The Mid-Canada Line itself had been a mere short-lived blip in the bigger defensive scheme. Being the most useful, the DEW Line hung on the longest; officially shut down as late as 1993, it has continued in another form and under another name electronically spanning the Arctic and keeping an eye on whatever might come from across the North Pole. Now known as the North Warning System (NWS), it has, because of aforesaid technology's relentless advance, far fewer sites and far fewer people to keep it going than did its predecessor. Unlike the DEW Line, however, the NWS has even less presence culturally. The DEW Line may have epitomized the Cold War and had some presence in popular culture courtesy its association with Buckminster Fuller's useful geodesic domes, but the NWS registers not at all. The vast majority of people have no idea that it even exists. Out of sight, out of mind.

So the Cold War petered out in the late 1980s as American President Ronald Reagan's dream of a so-called Star Wars missile defence system effectively bankrupted the Soviet Union while they tried to keep pace with American military spending. My father finally came home, one of the last hard-core DEW Liners to leave as the system underwent its transformation and rebranding. Much like the world to the south, his world in the Arctic had changed beneath his feet, and he spent the last couple of years up there shuttling back and forth across the Line, moving from station to station, presumably (for I'm only able to make guesses based on what little he said of it all) helping make the transition orderly. Everything back in North Bay had changed immensely during the years he was gone; the home I lived in through most of my high-school years was a house he'd never lived in, only visited during his yearly leaves, sometimes not even staying there but rather at a nearby motel. I don't know exactly why he came back, nor do I know why my mother took him back. After everything that had happened, did she still somehow love him? Did she feel some obligation to the father of her children? Was there guilt? Though they'd had a formal separation agreement since his departure in the fall of 1969, she'd never made the ultimate break, never divorced him, never remarried. So I can't help but wonder: was it the Catholic in her? I have such a lack of understanding of the human heart – of, especially, my mother's heart – that I quickly encounter the very limits of my comprehension and can go no further. My father may (and please note that qualifier, as it is important) be an easier study: he was old and broken, and I think he had nowhere else to go.

Of the fitting ironies that characterize my relationship with him, one of the biggest has to be the fact that he came home pretty much just in time to watch me leave. I departed North Bay for good in 1990 after years of trying to make it feel like home and failing time and again. Having no real model to work from, I suppose that was inevitable. From my father I had learned the basics of being a misfit, and had gone on to perfect it all on my own. But I sometimes wonder if the anger I'd allowed to build within me through my teenage years had, as I became an adult, ossified and hardened into something like an impermeable exoskeleton of resentment that precluded the ability to connect with a place – and especially with North Bay and the anger calcified there. Since I didn't and couldn't ever confront my father about anything I ever felt, in one way or another perhaps I took it out on North Bay, holding it in some weird way accountable for my misery. Ultimately, I wonder if it could never be home because I simply wouldn't allow it.

So after a twenty-seven-year absence, I returned to Nova Scotia to live in Halifax. Two days after arriving there I drove out the twenty-five miles to see Beaverbank – or what was left of it – for the first time since we'd left in the spring of 1963. I was surprised that so much of it was still extant, including the miserable PMQ in which we'd lived and the decaying concrete stoop out back on which I had learned to tie my shoes, watched the *Golden Hawks* roar overhead, prepared for another toboggan run down our tier and across the field …

I began, but then turned my back on, the mile-long walk up the road to the operation site where the base's radar domes had been situated and where my father had spent his workdays. I hadn't seen them as a child when we lived on the base – was, in fact, picked up and taken back home by a couple of military-police officers driving a jeep the one time I did try to make my way up the road – and decided, in the end, that some mysteries of my childhood were perhaps better left that way. The domes were long gone, and maybe it was best not to shatter at least one of the myths of my memory with the ugly truth of abandoned and decaying concrete and metal. So I turned my back on the place, returning only briefly in the fall of 2001 to show my wife, Heather (herself an army brat), where I came from, arriving in time to witness the foundation for a new home being poured where our PMQ had once stood. My grief surprised me.

Back in North Bay a few years after my departure, my father's health had begun its inexorable deterioration. Now in his seventies, Alzheimer's disease began to show its ugly face. (When I heard the diagnosis during a telephone call with my mother, I couldn't help but recall a story he had told me years earlier about the caches of canned beer left by the yearly Sealift operation. As supplies ran low in the months before the next summer's resupply, the remaining cans of beer would taste so strongly of aluminium that the very taste of the beverage itself was obliterated. It reminded me of a once-posited link between aluminum and Alzheimer's disease.) Around the same time my father was diagnosed with prostate cancer. On my rare visits home, he was a shadowy figure who did his best to stay at the margins socially, reading the newspaper, playing solitaire on the computer, watching golf and the occasional wedding show (which I saw brought tears to his eyes, overwhelming me with a helplessness and grief that would force me to take refuge in the bathroom to hide my own). He began to have trouble walking, and increasingly took to using canes and then a wheelchair. On one visit home, my mother pressed me into getting him out of the house and taking him to a coffee shop at a nearby mall. Her hope was connected less, I think, with getting us to somehow connect and more with simply wanting to get him out of her hair for a little while. So, pushing him in his wheelchair, off we went. Once there, I left him at a table and went to get our coffee, desperately trying to think of something innocuous we could talk about when I came back. As it turned out,

I needn't have bothered. He took his cup from me, drained it, and said he was ready to go home.

During a visit a couple of years before his death, I saw the deterioration of his mind beginning to show. He called me by his brother's name, correcting himself with great frustration, and referred to my youngest sister Renee by his youngest sister's name. Sitting and watching golf with him one afternoon, he turned to me to say something. I looked at him from across the room, his eyes on me, his lips open to speak. I waited. But the words never came. He finally waved me away in frustration. Was it Alzheimer's that denied him the words, or the equally insidious disease of silence that had always been our common ground? Was it the new disease, or the old one? Whichever, we never found a way past it, and I was as equally complicit in its ultimate success as was my father. I was a good student – I learned some things from him – but I never grew enough to develop the courage to try and push past what I had learned and attempt to forge some meaningful connection with this man. Our only bond, it seemed, was the inability to speak any truths to one another. All we seemed to share was the absence of a common vocabulary.

Increasingly, he had trouble swallowing food, and so a feeding tube had been installed into his stomach through which he could take liquid nutrition. I watched my mother work the system and one evening boldly asked if I could take over. My mother was more than willing to let someone else try, and to my amazement my father agreed. The first step in the process involved hooking up a syringe of cold water to the tube so as to clear it out. But I hadn't learned the intricacies of the process and forced the water in too fast. My father jumped as the shock of cold water hit him, which made us both laugh. I relaxed a bit and managed to hook him up to the bag of beige liquid that would ooze slowly into his stomach over the course of the next hour. That was the last time I would hear my father's laugh, and one of the very rare occasions when we did it together.

In the fall of 1997, a year before he died, I had moved from Nova Scotia to Prince Edward Island to take a job at the Confederation Centre Art Gallery in Charlottetown, and early the following summer I managed to see him briefly one last time. In the last couple of months before his death, my sister Danielle put her own life and family on hold and went home to help my mother. We all knew what was coming, and my father eventually took some control over what was left of his life, and a week before his death, stopped taking food altogether.

I spoke with my mother on the phone each evening, foolishly struggling to find the right timing, the right flight home, not knowing how long he'd last. I think that I was, in fact, stalling, afraid to face him in the end, afraid of what we might say, maybe more afraid of the sureness of what we could not bring ourselves to say; maybe afraid of his remote, seemingly judgmental silence, afraid of my inability to bridge the gap between us, afraid he might just dismiss me with another wave of his hand ...

Just afraid.

The morning I was finally scheduled to fly out of Charlottetown was the morning he died, August 31, 1998. My mother called with the news in the small hours of the morning, just as I was headed out the door. Did I want to see his body before it was cremated, she asked?

No.

I arrived home late that evening, after my exhausted mother and sister had gone to bed. I sat downstairs watching TV for a while. I couldn't bring myself to go into what had once been my bedroom but which had become his, and stood staring at the closed

Plaque at National Air Force Museum, Trenton

door wondering what might be on its far side, imagining the still rumpled sheets of his death bed, the dent in the pillow where his head would have lain as he died ... I slept that night on the couch in the family room, and when I opened the door to the bedroom in the braver light of morning, it was totally cleaned out, devoid of rumples, dents, and monsters. Even the hospital bed he'd used had already been taken away.

At the funeral a few days later, it was my father's military life that people saw: medals, patches, and rank insignia all laid out beside his enlistment photograph plus the hat that was part of his last uniform. The ex-military father of a friend who had seen the awesome flotilla of the D-Day invasion from high above the English Channel in the bomber he was navigating back to England after a night mission over Germany came up to me afterwards. He explained to me the meaning and significance of the seemingly abstract strokes of colour on a long, thin bar of cloth called a Decoration Ribbon, but in the daze of my grief it was another fact that didn't stick in my memory. During the service my youngest sister spoke publicly of her grief at his passing and her anger at his absence from her life as she grew up.

I held Heather's hand and said nothing.

After the funeral, we drove down to the shore of Lake Nipissing, walked out to the end of a long municipal dock, and, standing atop some large boulders that formed a breakwater, spread some of his ashes on the choppy waters. My mother had asked me to go with her to Windsor and spread the remainder on the Detroit River, but I was still living in Charlottetown and kept finding reasons and excuses not to do it. So the following summer, tired of waiting for me, she and my sisters went out onto Lake Nipissing by boat and spread what was left of his ashes across its water. I felt surprisingly free of guilt, finding it comforting to think his dust would wend its way through the watershed that drained Lake Nipissing through the French River into Lake Huron's Georgian Bay, south through Lake St. Clair and eventually flow into his beloved Detroit River.

He would go home again.

~

I guess I'm supposed to have learned something from all of this by now, managed to come to terms with my father at long last. I originally began writing about my father simply as an exercise in remembering. Small shards of memory would drift up into my consciousness and roll around in my mind as I examined them from many angles. When I finally let them go, I would wonder whether these memories would slip back beneath the surface, never to be heard from again. So I started this as an exercise, just jotting down memories as they broke the surface in an effort to merely keep them afloat. But as details began to accumulate, as the shards and slivers of remembrances began to coalesce into something of form, shape, and substance, I thought that maybe, just maybe, I could somehow piece together the person who was my father – I could reconstruct him and set him to walking and talking again, to ask him the questions to which I so very badly needed answers. Maybe, I thought, I could figure out who this man really was and where I belonged in his life. Maybe he would finally tell me.

Such a load of maybes. Such hubris. I've learned nothing. My father remains as elusive as he had always been, slipping through my fingers like sand. No, more like quicksilver – like stave-offish mercury that mixes with virtually nothing yet is readily absorbed through the skin, that reveals nothing about itself, its shiny surface offering only reflections of the world about it. Is that the simile I want: my father, liquid mercury? A toxic substance? Inadequate, but I guess it will have to do.

And there is The Box, sitting beneath my desk. Sometimes I feel like it taunts me as I obsessively root around within it, poring over my father's photographs, pulling out a magnifying glass and focusing on the relatively few images in which he allowed himself to be included, hoping that *this* time I will be able to read him, become privy to whatever his face is telling me, whatever his body language might be suggesting. And I read and reread the photocopied pages of his military record, hoping to dredge up something I've previously missed, some critical bit of information that will turn out to be the key that will finally open up my father's life before me.

It's all for nought. In The Box and in the pile of bureaucratic paperwork that constitutes his military record, I've foolishly sought a kind of redemption from mutely inert things. But these are little more than the official record of what passed for the public man. They're silent. They're dead. Even the photographs I so treasure are all about the mask(s) of his professional, working life and they tell me squat about the private man, about the interior workings that evaporated on August 31, 1998, as, a thousand miles away in the darkness of the early pre-dawn hours, I finished packing my bags, drank my morning coffee, and dried my hair. I had had my chance. Actually, I had so very many of them. I could have asked him questions, been persistent, rebuffed his rebuffing, pestered, even nagged him towards something of a response. Maybe I could have been biblical; maybe I could have been like Jacob wrestling through an Old Testament night with God, refusing to release him – my father – until I received a blessing. Maybe this is what I should have said to him, to my father: *I will not let you go until you bless me.*

But I didn't. I've merely racked up a lot of maybes, lacking the courage to truly wrestle with my father for answers to questions I needed to ask when I had the chance, lacking the willingness to find or even build a vocabulary we could share. I was afraid to risk further injury, to be denied honesty. I chose, instead, riskless-ness. I chose to shield myself from whatever might have been the truth about him and about our relationship, excused myself from confronting his will to silence head-on. In the end, I opted for the familiarity of his/my/*our* default mode: saying nothing.

~

So it was, for the most part, with my sisters. The fact is that neither before nor after my father's death did my three sisters and I ever speak about our lives with one another, tell each other of how we each experienced the anguishes and joys of our lives as itinerant military brats. Perhaps the two older of my sisters did; growing up, they had always shared a bedroom and so perhaps the exchanges took place between them there. But it's something I never spoke with them about, nor they with me. We never traded experiences, shared our pain. We never spoke of it at all. It was as if we lived in our own little cocoons of memories and pain, sealed off from one another. There is an emotional void, here, that spans my family. Did I help make it so? I gave my sister Danielle an early version of one of the chapters of this book to check against her memory, and ended up inadvertently inducing trauma as she was forced to revisit her own childhood pain. Therapeutic, maybe, but not what I had intended or, perhaps naively, even expected. My oldest sister Elizabeth's response was, for the longest time, silence.

And there is my youngest sister and my problematic

relationship with her. Born during our posting to Tacoma, she was but a year old when we moved east across the continent to North Bay. She has no memories of Tacoma, none of our difficult trip from that posting to our final one back in Canada. So she has no experience of being a military brat, and maybe that fact set the initial width of a distance between us.

She was nine years old when I left to attend university, and the gap inevitably widened, though I never thought about it at the time. In many ways I became for her the sibling equivalent of our father: showing up periodically – for, say, the summer months, and then gone again after usually just eating and sleeping at home and having little to do with my family as I indulged in a brief spell of sociability that spanned the last year of high school and the years of university. While I had read her bedtime stories when she was two and three years old, babysat her in the family car as my mom, dad, and other two sisters picked blueberries in the bush outside North Bay, and while the ten-year-old me had rinsed her poopy diapers before they were sterilized and washed (a duty I did unquestioningly, to my wife's continued astonishment, though I keep telling her there was never any option of doing otherwise), this is stuff she was too young to remember. She doesn't remember when I was a brother to her, but she does remember when I wasn't. In the bigger picture, I ended up not being much of family to the adolescent, teenager, and adult she became. The consequence of that, of course, is that she was never much of family to me.

This is a lesson I've just learned – right now, as I write this at twenty minutes after seven on the evening of Sunday, March 7, 2010. Had I been smarter and known earlier that this would be an inevitable family dynamic, I might have had a chance to rescue not only my relationship with my youngest sister, but perhaps worked up the courage to at least try and seek some common ground, some shared language, with my father during his life. It's been so much easier to make a sort of peace with the dead man, to find something resembling common ground now – to, in fact, force it upon him because he cannot turn away from me now. I wrestle with his afterimage still, and though it has become easier over time, I know I will never now hear a blessing.

I'm a middle-aged man, and I learn all of this now, just as I write these words down. I've long known from my professional work writing about visual art that I find what I feel and understand about, say, a sculpture, drawing, or painting only in the actual process of writing about it. But this is the first time I've written about my family, hence, I guess, the delayed lessons of life as only now does the dynamic become so much clearer and more meaningful; only now does the pattern that connects us yet simultaneously keeps us apart pop up out of all the background rubbish and noise that fills my mind and sets my guts into turmoil.

~

All through those years of growing up a military brat, those years of transfers and moves from base to base, what I really needed (and I will extrapolate from my experience and say that it is what my sisters needed as well) was to be weighed down, to be held close to some piece of earth somewhere so as to be able to send out roots and locate myself, to become a part of a place and so find out who I was and how long-lasting, sustainable relationships with other human beings might be built. There was, of course, always the desire on our part for weight; there was always the need on our part for closeness and attachment to some small patch of place, to other people. But there wasn't a hope in hell that it would ever happen. The imperatives of the Cold War meant that, for families like mine (and we were and are by no means unique) such privileges could not be permitted. There could be no weight, no heaviness to hold us in place and allow us grow, to attach. We would go where we were needed – where my father, as small a bit player as he was in all of this enormous geopolitical structure, was needed. His weightless family would consequently follow.

Such experiences inevitably leave their mark. Families of course disintegrate under the pressure. Drugs and alcohol become coping mechanisms (and I was surprised back in the late 1970s of how casually my father spoke of the drugs that made their way to the DEW Line, though as a dedicated alcoholic they held no interest for him). People struggle to learn how to find the weight that will hold them to a place and allow them to grow, and so often they fail. Like me. The poet and monk Thomas Merton wrote: "it is important to know where you are put on the face of the earth." Yes.

Oh, yes.

Sometime around my father's final return from the Arctic I acquired his magnetic compass. I can't remember exactly when or how, but it came into my possession and I have it still. It's a very good-quality piece of technology. Manufactured by the German company Lutz, it has the degrees precisely marked around the compass and one very odd feature I've never been able to find an explanation for and which I've never seen on another such device: East and West are reversed. North is true, though, and every place I've lived since it came into my possession – North Bay, Halifax, Charlottetown, and now Colborne – it sits atop a bookcase shelf, the needle pointing me the way north.

"I am a traveller like all my fathers," reads Psalm 39:12 of the

Hebrew Bible. That's me. Feeling rootedness and experiencing a sense of place are things that didn't happen for me until I was in my late forties, when I moved to Colborne, married the woman I was truly meant to spend my life with, and struggled once more with where I was. I didn't expect we would be here long – both my wife and I left other lives and careers in other places to come here only to care for her aging and ill mother – and I fully expected that we would eventually be free to move on somewhere else. And so for the first two years I actively resisted this place. Hated it, in fact. I hadn't the set of skills needed to become a part of this tiny little corner of the planet, and so I flailed about uselessly in total frustration. It was only through the miracle of my marriage that I learned of closeness and real commitment that rooted us within one another – in short, learned the truths of love – and so slowly, incrementally, began to root myself in this place, learning to allow the rolling rural landscape of Northumberland County in this part of southeastern Ontario to actually seep into me, become a part of who I am slowly becoming. So when my mother-in-law died, we stayed on. We planted trees in memory of our parents, nourished them, and watched them grow. As an early-morning riser, I would sit in the dark and watch for the dawn as it touched upon this spot of our planet, witnessing each morning how and exactly where the eastern horizon would begin to glow.

Daybreak.

~

When you live in the Arctic, you need a good coat.

My father's last parka is a forty medium. The exterior shell is waterproofed green canvas, the interior lining copper coloured.

It's stuffed full of goose down. It reaches the knees, and both inside and out has numerous pockets. In addition to two large pockets at the hips, there are slits high up in the chest area into which hands can be slipped and protected. The arms have cuffs that seal tightly around the wrists. The detachable hood is fur trimmed. It has both a large zipper and large buttons – attached not by thread but rather sturdy canvas loops – which cold fingers can easily manipulate.

I'm really not sure if it ever made it to the Arctic. In the nearly twenty years my father spent up there, he would have gone through several coats. And while I know he took good care of his belongings, this one is in such fine shape I'm not sure he ever took it north. Still, there is some wear: the label is almost unreadable, the exterior pockets have rubbed edges that have worn away the coat's green colouring, and the Velcro fastening of the interior waistband that can be closed tightly to seal the body from the harsh elements has some of my father's silver hair caught up in it. Maybe I'm wrong.

What I do know for sure is that this was his last winter coat, his last parka. After his death, it was given to me along with some of his other clothing. But I have trouble wearing it. Oh, it fits just fine, and indeed some winter occasions call for such a good coat (in the late 1990s while still living on Prince Edward Island, I once wore it during a blizzard). But I think I don't want to wear it because I don't want it to die. I don't want to wear it out like I have his other clothing passed along to me. I don't want to lose this, which is I guess why I still hang on to his old worn-out briefcase from his DEW Line days. He wore the one, and carried the other. I need them both to sustain me on my trip.

And once I had a need for anger to sustain me. I suppose it was how I defined myself, tried to free myself from my father's shadow, such as it was. In so many ways it kept me going, gave me something to respond to, fight against – a wall to push against. So I spent a good portion of my life being angry with him – angry for ripping us from our home to move to somewhere else; angry for what I saw and felt as abandonment; angry, even, for how he would lavish affection and attention on my youngest sister Renee on his trips home from the DEW Line while not paying me much mind. I stewed and simmered with resentment over the love he showered upon her, yet at the same time wanted to escape his attention entirely, for I knew he would criticize the length of my hair, my clothing, my choice of music … I wanted affectionate attention and yet self-consciously dreaded its very possibility. My world was a tangle of teenage angst and plain old immaturity, and consequently very much of it was unfairly directed at the nearest available target: my father. Despite his legal separation from my mother when he went north to the DEW Line in 1969, he never financially abandoned us, his family. We were never in want, never in any kind of financial need. I grew up fortunate that way, and I cannot be angry for that.

And while I angrily accused him of it (though never to his face), the fact is that he never abandoned me emotionally, something I've had to come to terms with grudgingly – you know, with a lot of proverbial kicking and screaming. I wanted certain things from him – love and respect being the biggies – but it's taken me most of my adulthood to understand, to *really* understand, that I have wanted those things strictly on my terms. My inability to grasp this fact helped maintain the gulf of noncommunication between us, and undoubtedly poisoned me to the degree that I've been unable to maintain so many friendships begun and then abandoned for whatever reason. I have some understanding, now, of what it means when Old Testament Yahweh visits the sins of the fathers upon their sons, and their sons, etc. For good or ill (and so often the latter), we carry in our hearts the patterns of our parents, make the same mistakes, take the same self-destructive paths through our lives. Or, we simply react and reject. Me, I'm both of those people, moulded by fear and tending to reject before I'm rejected. So many of the wounds I lay at my father's feet are, in fact, self-inflicted. I have had legitimate anger at him, but it only resulted in the warping and twisting of my soul as I tried to build a life within the inferno of that fire. But the flames have died, the ashes cooled, and I've begun at last to build something that will last. This is me: Gil McElroy, phoenix.

So here, let me end with one of the last pictures ever taken of my father, the image that begins this chapter. One of my nieces took it during a visit. It's an appropriate image because it fits the man: difficult to completely make out against the setting in which he is in, just like so many of my memories of him. The image is washed out by the light from a window and door in the kitchen against which my father is framed, caught rising with difficulty from the kitchen table, leaning on the two canes that he needed to help him move about, beginning the long process of making his way slowly back to the family room where he will read the paper. Alone. He'll be dead within a year.

This is how it ends: his death, and the long, sometimes painful, often surprising trek I've made towards what, for most people, would be a not-all-that-profound realization that, in the only way of which I think he was capable, my father was in fact always there for me. In the midst of the self-absorption of my simmering rage and resentment, I was unable to see it or allow myself to feel it. But once, just once, something broke through. In the mid-1980s, quite out of the blue, he sent me a card from the Arctic – not, though, to my address but care of my mother's – with a small cheque. The money is long gone. It was a nice gift to receive, and as I recall very useful at the time. But it was fleeting and ultimately not all that consequential to the big picture of my life.

But the card was. It still is. Through all the moves in my life from one place and home to another that followed its arrival, I've managed to hold on to it. It lives in The Box, now. Inside it, in the neat printing of the draftsman that he had once been and that I would recognize anywhere (and that I had often tried unsuccessfully to emulate), my father calls me "my only beloved son."

I have it in writing.

10

AFTER THE WAR

After the war, there's this one final image.

I don't even know if it's his, if he took it. It hung in the living room of my family's home for years, and now it hangs in mine. It's the only one of his photographs he ever had professionally framed. If it's his.

Though I want it to be so, unknowing must leave it a blank.

But here is its equivalent in seventeen words: six polar bears swim together away from the camera through chunks of ice in an Arctic sea.

Is that enough?

He loved this picture, loved the fact of its unusualness. Polar bears never swim together in such groups, he would say, never gather together like this. It's probably two females and their young, together. Solitary creatures, male and female bears would only come together for mating. The female would then raise the young alone, the male driven off for the threat he posed them.

That's enough.

NOTES

In Chapter 2, Chain Home (Triad), information about the Pinetree Line is from the website of the late Ren L'Ecuyer, who founded and maintained the Pinetree Line website until his death in 2007, after which his wife Margaret took over for several years. L'Ecuyer superbly documented all the World War II Chain Home sites on both the Pacific and Atlantic using both archived military files and personal recollections by those who served on them.

Hilda Glynn-Ward's *The Writing on the Wall: In Three Parts Past, Present and Future* was originally released by Sun Publishing of Vancouver in 1921. In 1974 it was republished by the University of Toronto Press with a contextualizing introduction by historian Patricia E. Roy.

The story about Donald Scratch and the stolen B-25 entitled "Airman Terrorises District in Wild Flight in Bomber" appeared on page 1 of the December 11, 1944, edition of *The Advertiser* in Adelaide, Australia. It was also reported in the *Globe and Mail.* More recently, *Airforce Magazine* published the article "The Last Flight of Donald Scratch" by Pat MacAdam in its Winter 2008 issue (Vol. 31, No. 4).

In Chapter 3, Yellow Beetle, the Government of Ontario formally designated the section of Highway 401 between Trenton and Toronto (where the body of every soldier killed in Afghanistan was taken upon arrival in Canada to the Centre for Forensic Sciences) by the additional name "*Highway of Heroes*" in August 2007.

In Chapter 4, Sugarcane (Yellowjack), the photograph of my father and other instructors at Clinton in 1951 was found on the fighter control operators (FCO) website. The site contains numerous course photographs of both instructors and graduates taken over the years at Clinton. See *Further Reading* for the website particulars.

The ability of the U-2 to fly at very high altitude was supposed to keep it safe from Soviet interceptor jets and missiles that had difficulty functioning in the thin air at such height. The downing by a plane flown by CIA pilot Francis Gary Powers in May 1960 by a Soviet surface-to-air missile embarrassingly and clearly demonstrated just how quickly the Soviets technologically caught up.

In Chapter 5, Pinetree (Midwife / Redtape), travel by ship was the usual way the RCAF moved its personnel and their dependents between Canada and overseas postings until the early 1960s, when European postings started to be done using commercial air carriers.

The Pinetree, DEW, and Mid-Canada Lines were in very large part about the protection of the industrial heartland that was then located in the lower forty-eight states of the United States. Even more importantly, they were also built to protect USAF Strategic Air Command bases then situated deep in the continental United States from which U.S. bombers carrying retaliatory nuclear weapons would be flown towards their Soviet targets, refuelled en route from flying tankers stationed at USAF bases situated in Newfoundland.

For an interesting fact-based fictional account of life for nonmarried personnel on a remote Pinetree Line site, see Peter Garland's *Permanent Echoes*.

In Chapter 6, Mid-Canada, the occasional reference to the Mid-Canada Line as the "McGill Fence" was based on the fact that much of the technology that made the system operationally possible was developed at McGill University in Montreal.

To be fair, the Doppler radar system of the Mid-Canada Line was designed *not* to be triggered by incidents like a bunch of Canada Geese flying within detection range of its towers, though migratory birds in fact posed a huge detection headache. But I've read the web-posted words of a reminiscing radar technician who worked there, saying, "We either got nothing or we got geese, we never, ever got aircraft. It was a hopeless system." See Larry Wilson's Mid-Canada Line website.

In Chapter 8, Distant Early Warning, the military base at North Bay shared its long runway with commercial flights; it was not uncommon to see Boeing 747 passenger jets practising takeoffs and landings there. In 1977, Merle Dickerson, a colourful mayor of the period, attempted to capitalize upon the presence of a massive runway in a public relations stunt ostensibly intended to lure the then-new Concorde supersonic airliner to use North Bay as its North American terminus after it was initially denied landing rights in New York.

Statistics I used for the construction of the DEW Line are taken from *The Distant Early Warning (DEW) Line Marks 25 Years on Watch*, published by FELEC Services to commemorate the Line's Silver Anniversary in 1982.

In Chapter 9, Parka, the destruction of the Berlin Wall resulted in my owning a small chunk of it, won for correctly answering a political question posed by the shortwave broadcaster Radio Deutsche Welle.

The Tiananmen Square massacre I heard on shortwave radio and watched on television caused such anguish it drove me out into the streets of North Bay to protest in front of the office of the local MP with a homemade sign. I could think of nothing else to do. Apparently, a lot of people who saw me thought I was a radical anti-abortionist.

The Kol Israel shortwave broadcast occurred on the evening (in North America) of January 17, 1991.

FURTHER READING

BOOKS

Barris, Ted. *Behind the Glory: The Plan that Won the Allied Air War.* Toronto: Macmillan Canada, 1992.

British Commonwealth Air Training Plan: 60th Anniversary, The. Ottawa: Veterans Affairs Canada, 2000.

Buderi, Robert. *The Invention that Changed the World: How a Small Group of Radar Pioneers Won the Second World War and Launched a Technological Revolution.* New York: Simon & Schuster, 1996.

Clearwater, John. *Canadian Nuclear Weapons: The Untold Story of Canada's Cold War Arsenal.* Toronto: Dundurn, 1998.

———. *U.S. Nuclear Weapons in Canada.* Toronto: Dundurn, 1999.

Coates, Ken S., P. Whitney Lackenbauer, William R. Morrison, and Greg Poelzer. *Arctic Front: Defending Canada in the Far North.* Toronto: Thomas Allen, 2008.

Conant, Jennet. *Tuxedo Park: A Wall Street Tycoon and the Secret Palace of Science that Changed the Course of World War II.* New York: Simon & Schuster, 2002.

Conant, Melvyn. *The Long Polar Watch: Canada and the Defense of North America.* New York: Harper & Brothers, 1962.

Conn, Stetson, Rose C. Engleman, and Bryon Fairchild. *Guarding the United States and Its Outposts.* Washington, DC: Center of Military History, United States Army, 1964. Online at www.history.army.mil/books/wwii/guard-US/.

De Landa, Manuel. *War in the Age of Intelligent Machines.* New York: Zone Books, 1991.

Dickson, Frances Jewel. *The DEW Line Years: Voices From the Coldest Cold War.* East Lawrencetown, NS: Pottersfield Press, 2007.

Distant Early Warning (DEW) Line Marks 25 Years on Watch, The. Colorado Springs: FELEC Services, Inc., 1982.

Douglas, William (W.A.B.). *The Creation of a National Air Force: The Official History of the Royal Canadian Air Force,* Vol. 3. Toronto: University of Toronto Press, 1986.

Dunmore, Spencer. *Wings for Victory: The Remarkable Story of the British Commonwealth Air Training Plan in Canada.* Toronto: McClelland & Stewart, 1994.

Dwiggins, Don. *The Complete Book of Airships: Dirigibles, Blimps, and Hot Air Balloons.* Blue Ridge Summit, PA: TAB Books, 1980.

English, Allan, and Colonel John Westrop (retired). *Canadian Air Force Leadership and Command: The Human Dimension of Expeditionary Air Force Operations.* Ottawa: Department of National Defence, 2007.

Garland, Peter. *Permanent Echoes.* London, ON: Third Eye, 1991.

Gray, David R. *Beyond the Inuit Lands: The Story of Canadian Forces Station Alert.* Ottawa: Borealis Press, 2004.

Guide to McChord. Tacoma, WA: Armed Forces Directory Service, 1962.

Hart, Elisa, and Cathy Cockney. *Yellow Beetle Oral History and Archaeology Project.* Report prepared for the Inuvialuit Social Development Program, March 1999.

Joint Press Tour, Distant Early Warning (DEW) Line, March 26–April 3, 1956. Royal Canadian Air Force, Western Electric, United States Air Force.

Kuznick, Peter J., and James Gilbert, eds. *Rethinking Cold War Culture.* Washington, DC: Smithsonian Institution Press, 2001.

Leach, Norman S. *Broken Arrow: America's First Lost Nuclear Weapon.* Calgary: Red Deer Press, 2008.

Lindsey, George R., ed. *No Day Long Enough: Canadian Science in World War II.* Toronto: Canadian Institute of Strategic Studies, 1997.

Maloney, Sean M. *Learning to Love the Bomb: Canada's Nuclear Weapons During the Cold War.* Washington, DC: Potomac Books, Inc., 2007.

McConnell, David. *Plan for Tomorrow ... Today! The Story of Emergency Preparedness Canada, 1948–1998.* Ottawa: Heritage Research Associates, 1998.

McDougall, Walter A. *The Heavens and the Earth: A Political History of the Space Age.* New York: Basic Books, 1985.

Middleton, W.E. Knowles. *Radar Development in Canada: The Radio Branch of the National Research Council of Canada, 1939–1946.* Waterloo, ON: Wilfred Laurier University Press, 1981.

Milberry, Larry. *Canada's Air Force at War and Peace,* Vol. 3. Toronto: CANAV Books, 2001.

NBC Group, The (Don Nicks, John Bradley, Chris Charland). *A History of the Air Defence of Canada 1948–1997.* Ottawa: Commander Fighter Group, 1997.

Norris, Kathleen. *Acedia and Me: A Marriage, Monks, and a Writer's Life.* New York: Riverhead Books, 2008.

Ozorak, Paul. *Abandoned Military Installations of Canada,* Vol. 1, *Ontario.* Self-published, 1991.

Rens, Jean-Guy. *The Invisible Empire: A History of the Telecommunications Industry in Canada, 1846–1956.* Montreal, QC, and Kingston, ON: McGill-Queen's University Press, 2001.

Vance, Jonathan F. *High Flight: Aviation and the Canadian Imagination.* Toronto: Penguin Canada, 2002.

Watson-Watt, Sir Robert. *Three Steps to Victory: A Personal Account by Radar's Greatest Pioneer.* London: Odhams Press, 1957.

EXHIBITION CATALOGUE

Fortier, Rénald. *The R.100 in Canada.* National Aviation Museum, 1999.

ARTICLES AND ESSAYS

"Arctic Log." *Western Electric Magazine*, November–December 1955.

Boyne, Walter J. "The Rise of Air Defense." *Air Force Magazine*, Vol. 82, No. 12 (December 1999), www.afa.org/magazine/1299rise.html.

"Continental Defense." *Western Electric Magazine*, July–August 1955.

"DEW Line Ceremonies Mark Network Completion," *Bell Laboratories Record*, October 1957.

Earnest, Lee, Jim Wong, Paul Edwards, "Vigilance and Vacuum Tubes: The SAGE System 1956–63." www.computerhistory.org/events/lectures/sage_051998/sage_xscrpt.shtml.

"First DEW Building Accepted by U.S. Air Force." *Bell Laboratories Record*, January 1957.

"First DEW Line Sites Turned Over to Air Force." *Bell Laboratories Record*, May 1957.

"Five Days on the DEW Line." *Western Electric Magazine*, January–February 1956.

"572." *Western Electric Magazine*, November–December 1953.

Fletcher, Roy J. "Military Radar Defence Lines of Northern North America." www.pinetreeline.org/resartg.html.

Gauthier, Don. "Concorde Is Welcome in N. Bay, Dickerson Says." *The North Bay Nugget*, Wednesday, March 9, 1977, 1.

Gauthier, Group Captain E.J. "Evolution of RCAF Telecommunications (Second of Three Parts: World War II)." *The Roundel*, Vol. 16, No. 10 (December 1964), 18–22.

Gooderham, Squadron Leader D., O.B.E. "So You're Going North?" *The Roundel*, Vol. 1, No. 10 (August 1949), 23–25.

Grant, Robert S. "Dewline Delivery." *Canadian Aviation*, Vol. 58, No. 11 (November 1985), 45–49.

Hall, Norm and Carol. "At a Crucial Hour: The Attack on Estevan Point." *The Beaver*, Vol. 84, No. 2 (April–May 2004), 18–24.

Harris, Lyndon T. (Bucky). "The DEWline Chronicles." www.magmacom.com/~lwilson/dewhist-a.htm.

Johnson, Arthur. "Undoing the DEW Line." *Canadian Geographic*, Vol. 127, No. 2 (March–April 2007), 62–72.

Kolbert, Elizabeth. "Dymaxion Man: The Visions of Buckminster Fuller." *The New Yorker*, June 9, 2008, www.newyorker.com.

La Fay, Howard. "DEW Line, Sentry of the Far North." *The National Geographic Magazine*, Vol. CXIV, No. 1 (July 1958), 128–46.

Ladurantaye, Steve. "Cold War Relic Gets Costly Cleanup." *Globe and Mail*, Friday, May 27, 2011, A9.

Limbrick, Wing Commander C.B. "Canada's Radar Outposts: A Little Known Chapter in the History of the R.C.A.F. during the Second World War." *The Roundel,* Vol. 2, No. 7 (May 1950), 39–42.

Martin, Capt. B. "Life on the DEW Line." *Canadian Forces Sentinel*, Vol. 4, No. 3 (March 1968), 24–27.

Neufeld, Dave. "Trigger for Atomic Holocaust Aircraft Detection on the DEW Line." www.stankievech.net/projects/DEW/BAR-1/BAR-1_articles.html.

"Next Door to S. Claus: Christmas on the D.E.W. Line: A Report on Winter Life in the Far North." *Western Electric Magazine*, November–December 1954.

Pang, Alex Soojung-Kim. "Dome Days: Buckminster Fuller in the Cold War." In *Cultural Babbage: Technology, Time and Invention*, Francis Sufford and Jenny Uglow, eds. London: Faber & Faber, 1996.

Paradis, Scott. "Abandoned Radar Bases Remain Toxic Legacy." *The North Bay Nugget,* Tuesday, July 31, 2007, www.nugget.ca.

Patriache, Group Captain V.N. "The Strategy of the Arctic." *The Roundel*, Vol. 2, No. 9 (April 1950), 38–42.

"SAGE Data Transmission Service." *Bell Laboratories Record*, October 1957.

Schwarz, Frederic D. "Sweet Loran." *American Heritage of Invention & Technology*, Vol. 23, No. 1 (Summer 2007), 8–9.

Stephenson, Michael. "The DEW Line." *The Beaver* (Winter 1983), 14–19.

"Thirty-Foot Antenna for the DEW Line." *Bell Laboratories Record*, November 1957.

Weicht, Chris. "Radio Detachments on the West Coast of Canada," www.pinetreeline.org/rds/detail/rds99-33.html.

Wolverton, Mark. "The DEW Line." *American Heritage of Invention & Technology*, Vol. 22, No. 4 (Spring 2007), 32–41.

WEBSITES

Canadian Wings: Unofficial website documenting the history of the Royal Canadian Air Force: www.canadianwings.com.

Pinetree Line: Official reports and photographs extensively documenting all the Pinetree Lines sites across Canada, as well as the Chain Home sites of World War II: www.pinetreeline.org (now defunct, but archived at http://web.archive.org/web/20080317104201/http://www.pinetreeline.org). Portions can also be found on the FCO News and Radomes websites.

Mid-Canada Line: Stories from and contacts for personnel who served on the Mid-Canada Line: www.lswilson.ca/mcl.htm.

FCO News: Website devoted to images and an extensive database of contacts for former Fighter Control Operators: www.oldfco.ca/fconews.

A Secret Landscape: Guide to Cold War infrastructure, the places and systems that helped protect North American security: http://coldwar-c4i.net/index.html.

Computer History: Includes background on "Whirlwind" and SAGE: www.computerhistory.org.

Radar History: Comprehensive coverage of radar history, from principles of operation to its use around the world: www.smecc.org/new_page_5.htm.

Electronic Encyclopedia of Civil Defense and Emergency Management: Research on the history, organization, and theory of civil defence and emergency management: http://facultystaff.richmond.edu/~wgreen/encyclopedia.htm.

Secrets of Radar Museum: Experiences, stories, and history of the men and women who helped build, develop, operate, maintain, and defend Canadian radar, here in Canada and abroad: www.secretsofradar.com/index.html.

BAR-1 DEW Line Archives: Comprehensive image archive for a section of the DEW (Distant Early Warning) radar chain that operated in the Yukon Territory, Canada: www.stankievech.net/projects/DEW/BAR-1/index.html.

McChord Air Force Base: Background information for the McChord base near Tacoma, Washington: www.mcchordairmuseum.org.

Online Air Defense Radar Museum: Wide-ranging website devoted to Cold War radar technology, sites, and personnel in the United States and Canada: www.radomes.org/museum.

INDEX

This index lists key places, projects, and topics related to the Cold War North America electronic defence network. **Boldface** indicates a photo caption.

G

H

I

J

K

L

M

S

T

ACKNOWLEDGEMENTS

Nothing happens in isolation, so I would like to extend my thanks to the following people who did so much towards making this book possible:

My mother, Ernestine Kircher McElroy
My sister, Danielle Brown
Jim Derham
The late Ren L'Ecuyer
Elisa Hart
Paul Ozorak
Ron Halal
Karl and Christy Siegler
Kevin Williams
Ann-Marie Metten
Gregory Gibson
Les Smith
Adam Swica
Stan Pankewich
Carol McArthur
Members of the Air Force Radar Sites Veterans web group
And Heather – for reading and rereading everything
as it was written

In memory of Donald Harrison McElroy
my father

and Michael Whatmore
my teacher

Photo: Courtesy the author

Born in Metz, France, poet Gil McElroy grew up on air force bases in Canada and the United States. He studied English Literature at Queen's University. His poems and other works have been published in numerous periodicals throughout North America since the late 1970s and issued in a number of self-published chapbooks, broadsheets, and one-of-a-kind book works. He has also published four full-length books of poetry with Talonbooks.

McElroy has also been an independent curator and freelance art critic for twenty years, organizing exhibitions for public art galleries and museums in Canada and writing art criticism for magazines in Canada, the United States, and Australia. A selection of his catalogue essays and reviews was published as *Gravity & Grace: Selected Writing on Contemporary Canadian Art* and in the anthology *CRAFT Perception and Practice: A Canadian Discourse*. His show *ST. ART: The Visual Poetry of bpNichol* pays tribute to one of the great poets of the twentieth century. Originally mounted at the Confederation Centre Art Gallery and Museum in Charlottetown, Prince Edward Island, in 2000, it later moved to the Art Gallery of Nova Scotia before touring the country throughout 2001. McElroy's curatorial essay accompanying the exhibition won the Christina Sabat Award for Critical Writing in the Arts.

Since 2007, McElroy has been collaborating with Halifax-based artist and curator Peter Dykhuis on a series of exhibitions collectively entitled Cold War Artifacts, each of which examines the social, economic, and cultural impact now-abandoned Cold War military installations had on their host communities. To date, exhibitions have been mounted in North Bay, Ontario, dealing with the squadron of nuclear-equipped missiles once stationed there; in Prince George, British Columbia, examining the impact of a Pinetree Line radar station near that community; and in Corner Brook, Newfoundland, dealing with an abandoned USAF military base in nearby Stephenville that would have been used to refuel nuclear-equipped bombers en route to targets in the former Soviet Union. Other exhibitions are planned.

McElroy lives in Colborne, Ontario, with his wife, Heather.